C000171436

A to Z

of

LEASING AND
ASSET FINANCE

Julian Rose & Stephen Bassett

2ND EDITION
revised and expanded

First published as a hardback original in 2017

This Second edition published in 2019

Copyright © Julian Rose & Stephen Bassett

The moral right of this author has been asserted.

Typeset in Adobe Garamond and Gotham Book

Design, editing, typesetting and publishing by UK Book Publishing

www.ukbookpublishing.com

ISBN: 978-1-912183-81-4

Contents

Foreword *1*

Introduction *5*

What is leasing? *6*

History *8*

A-Z of terms *12*

Index *164*

Abbreviations *185*

Short quiz *187*

Select Bibliography *193*

Asset Finance 50 .... *194*

Request for Input *198*

About the Authors *199*

Acknowledgements

Arkle Finance generously supported the publication of the first edition.

Terry Harvey, Ian Richmond, Leon Rose, Helena Thernstrom, Peter Thomas, Simon Trudgeon, and the team at Arkle Finance kindly suggested content for the first or second edition or reviewed certain terms. The efforts of all the contributors are greatly appreciated.

The authors are also grateful to readers of the first edition for their comments and suggestions. Any errors or omissions are the sole responsibility of the Authors.

Foreword

Since the first edition of the A-Z of Leasing and Asset Finance the asset finance and leasing industry has continued to enjoy strong levels of growth. The combination of good returns and a benign economy have attracted more new entrants to the sector and increased competition and innovation.

Importantly during this period, the industry has also made solid progress investing in younger talent and in their development. As an industry we still get a bad reputation for being "male, pale, and stale" but for me this is no longer a fair reflection of the industry we work in. The Leasing Foundation runs a networking event for young professionals which is always a sell-out event. There's been a real influx of new young professionals in asset finance who want to develop their skill set and build their network. Our industry has become more diverse in its makeup and this will become a key factor in helping us attract new talent in the future.

Some of the new young talent has come through the training academies of funders like Close and Hitachi Business Finance, others are completely new to the sector. The Finance and Leasing Association and the Leasing Foundation have both continued to provide training and development options to the next generation and we're starting to see a clearer framework and structure in this area which is really important. It is really encouraging to see that since 2016 over 150 people have signed up to study the FLA's Diploma in Asset Finance. This year the FLA has also had its Intermediate Leasing Course endorsed by the London Institute of Banking & Finance.

Another positive development has been Aldermore's training academy which is aimed at brokers, a section of the market which has historically been a breeding ground for new talent. This is a great example of a funder extending their training to the wider market and in turn supporting the development of next generation talent which helps all of us.

In 2019 The Leasing Foundation started a research programme to understand diversity and inclusion in business finance organisations. The research is part of their wider mission to help businesses understand the benefits of building diverse and inclusive teams, and to help embed inclusion and diversity into hiring, leadership development and learning.

Surveys show that millennial workers rate learning and development as an employee benefit much higher than cash bonuses. This doesn't necessarily mean making them sit through traditional module based training or writing down every aspect of their job in granular detail for them to read. Many Millennials went through school without reading a text book from start to finish. As an industry we also need to consider newer and more flexible training methods such as online courses, so maybe future editions of A-Z will be in digital formats as well as hard copy.

The MA in Leasing and Asset Finance by the Leasing Foundation is a great example of a flexible learning programme perfectly suited to the next generation as work related projects form the back bone of the programme. It focuses on innovation, disruption and changes in business finance which are relevant themes and will help influence change in our industry.

The latest edition of the A-Z has been extended to include new definitions as well as updates of existing ones. Wouldn't it be great if some new terms provided clarity around how leasing and asset finance is used to contribute to benefit customers and the importance of finance in well-functioning societies? The huge growth we've seen in energy efficient finance provides some great examples of this in terms of finance contributing towards a more sustainable future.

We need to show the importance of leasing and asset finance to a well-functioning economy and the wider society if we want to continue attracting the brightest new talent to our sector. To attract the very best we need to focus on communicating the principles and purpose of what we do and setting out the terminology of the industry is one element of this.

This book provides us with a clear explanation of the some of the more technical terms in finance and enables us to cut through the jargon. Most importantly it gets us all singing off the same hymn sheet and talking in a consistent way with customers. This in turn should make it easier for customers to understand our products and services. Every asset finance office should have one!

Nathan Mollett
Head of Asset Finance, Metro Bank and
Director, Leasing Foundation
December 2018

Foreword to the first edition

Where has all the training gone? That valuable insight from experts that passes on their knowledge and experience; that action of teaching that transfers skills and enables the student to competently execute their duties or tasks. It's fair to say that little has been done in our industry throughout the financial crisis to ensure the diligent transfer of knowledge and expertise. Arguably the lack of investment in the acquisition of those technical dimensions of what we do in Asset Finance and Leasing stretches back far beyond the onset of those dark days for financial services, with little written on the topic by industry sages since the late 90s.

It's clear to me that our industry has sustainability issues! Our population is getting older and, most worrying, those new participants lack the comprehensive training many of us received in our early careers with banks and finance houses. Thankfully – right on the cliff edge – we are all waking up to this point and much is being done across the industry to reverse the situation.

During my time at Aldermore, I have become acutely aware of the technical knowledge gap not only in my own new recruits but right across the introducer community. At Aldermore, we've focused heavily on filling those gaps – providing training in the fundamental principles of asset finance and additional modules covering regulation to hundreds of asset finance newbies.

It's encouraging to hear increasingly of the apprenticeships and academies supported by funders such as Hitachi Capital and Close Brothers as well as the efforts of the NACFB developing the skills of their membership, an increasingly important population in this market. Additionally we should all applaud the efforts of the Leasing Foundation and the Finance & Leasing Association who have crafted academic and development programmes of popular repute, tooling up our next generation with the vital knowledge and skills that enable asset finance and leasing to prosper in the future.

What we do – supporting business investment through lending – is still seen as an alternative source of finance for many; secondary to direct relationship lending by clearing Banks. That being said, awareness is increasing and our market is growing, reaching dizzy pre-crisis heights. Competency and skill in how we transact is a pre-requisite in this growing market and changing regulatory environment. Borrowers expect us to support them with precision and expertise. That's why the reinvigoration, perhaps better described as restoration, of critical knowledge transfer and training from industry experts is vital.

What better way to get everyone on the same page – speaking a common language and ensuring consistency in knowledge and understanding – than owning a well-regarded industry encyclopaedia, having it on your bookshelf not only as a reference guide but also an important enabler to universal education in the dark arts of asset finance and leasing.

Praise to Julian (and of course the Arkle Finance team) for pulling this comprehensive guide together with modern insight and the latest thinking.

Carl D'Ammassa
Group Managing Director – Business Finance, Aldermore Bank PLC
Former Chairman – Leasing Foundation
November 2016

Introduction

Equipment Leasing and Asset Finance explains the key concepts and techniques of this vital and significant part of the UK business finance market.

The scope spans the business and financial services environment in which the industry sits; the asset finance and leasing market and how it operates; the variety of agreement types which exist and the general legal and regulatory frameworks surrounding such agreements.

It is designed to assist everybody: from individuals within leasing companies; finance brokers; equipment suppliers and dealers who offer asset finance options; as well as those in the wider financial services market (including banks) who need to understand leasing solutions. It can also provide a valuable overview to those who are new to the market and a useful up-to-date reference guide for established practitioners.

The scope is framed as widely as possible. It encompasses any arrangements by which a finance company provides to another party a bailment, or the right of use, of the equipment or vehicles that it owns, under an agreement made between them.

The explanations describe the various ways in which some terms are used for different purposes, including for accounting (including the new IFRS 16), taxation, and in law and regulation.

Each definition is linked using *#hashtags* to one or more of twenty topics, spanning the business and financial services environment in which the industry operates, leasing operations, and the relevant legal and regulatory frameworks. The Index is sorted by topics, allowing the reader to review all associated terms together.

The new multi-choice quiz section is intended to help readers new to the industry to test their knowledge of a range of key terms.

Despite great care being taken, there will inevitably be some errors and omissions for which the authors accept full responsibility. Comments from readers will be very welcome and will be used to continually update, improve and refine the book in future editions.

What is leasing?

A good question!

Of all the terms in this book, perhaps one of the most difficult to define is the most fundamental one, i.e. 'leasing'. It is of such importance to the other terms in the book that it is repeated here.

The basics of leasing are very simple. In law, a leasing contract is a relationship of 'bailment', meaning there is a temporary transfer of assets from one person to another. Similarly, for accounting purposes under international accounting rules, a leasing contract gives the 'right of use' of an asset to another person.

So is any contract of 'bailment' in law, or one that provides the 'right of use' for accounting purposes, leasing?

In common use of the term 'leasing' it is usual to exclude short-term rentals from the definition of the leasing market. There is no clear line but bailments of less than 12 months are generally considered to be part of the short-term rental market rather than leases. Under the new international lease accounting standard, IFRS 16, lessees will have the option not to report leases of less than 12 months on their balance sheets.

It is common to focus on business, rather than individual consumer, leasing when discussing the leasing market. It is also common to include the services that often accompany the bailment of an asset.

Leasing is not a term defined in law and regulations. There are in fact a host of different types of bailment arrangements in common use. Some include the word 'lease', others – for example, hire purchase and conditional sale – do not. A traditional view, therefore, would be that leasing excludes these products. However, this does not fit with current accounting standards and neither is it fully aligned with tax rules, so it is actually useful to consider them as part of the wider leasing market.

It is probably useful to consider all bailment arrangements of similar characteristics as being part of the leasing market.

It is often proposed that it would be helpful to rename the market, perhaps as 'asset finance' or 'equipment finance' rather than 'leasing'. There is undoubtable merit in this idea but until all law and regulation on the subject is fully aligned there will always be a need to ask whoever is using any of these terms, precisely what they mean by them.

For this book, the term 'leasing' is the accounting one, hence we aim to include terms relevant to any form of bailment for business purposes other than short-term rentals.

History

Early development

The bailment of assets can be traced back to Babylonian law, with many of the legal principles in place today heavily influenced by Roman law.

Leasing, as a means of acquiring business capital assets, first developed significantly in the nineteenth century railway industry. One of the earliest leasing companies was the Birmingham Wagon Company, formed in 1854 to lease wagons to colliery owners. The North Central Wagon Company of Rotherham was founded in 1861, and still exists in the form of Lombard, part of the Royal Bank of Scotland.

Between the two world wars leasing was used by some machinery suppliers to restrict access to their new types of manufacturing equipment to customers willing to sign long-term lease commitments. In the UK the leasing industry then developed only slowly until the 1960s.

1960s

At this time some major specialist leasing companies set up in the UK, including the Mercantile Leasing Company, a joint venture of the United States Leasing Company and the Mercantile Credit Company.

Existing providers of hire purchase in the consumer credit market and some of the merchant banks, also established companies for the leasing of industrial equipment.

The industry grew strongly in the late 1960s as IBM, and later other computer companies, began to offer leasing options to their customers.

Lessors became eligible to claim investment grants on leased assets from 1966. Restrictions on the amount of credit that could be provided to non-bank leasing companies placed such companies at a disadvantage to bank and foreign lessors.

By the end of the 1960s around £100 million per year of new asset finance i.e. leasing and hire purchase provided to businesses was being arranged (£1.5bn today).

1970s

Following the introduction of tax capital allowances in 1970, the Government introduced 100 percent first year tax capital allowances in 1972. Leasing also became eligible for other forms of Government support intended to promote business investment. This all led to the steady expansion of the finance lease industry.

Leasing subsidiaries of clearing banks including Barclays, Williams & Glyn's and the Royal Bank of Scotland were set up to utilise the capital allowances, which were particularly valuable to the banks who were paying 52 percent tax on their profits.

The Consumer Credit Act 1974 replaced and expanded previous restrictions on, and regulation of the hire purchase industry. It extended regulation to hire and credit agreements provided to unincorporated businesses for values under £15,000.

By the end of the 1970s around £1.2 billion per year of new asset finance was being arranged (£6.2bn today).

1980s

The 1984 Finance Act scaled down capital allowances, with a maximum allowance of 25 percent per year on a reducing balance basis for most assets.

Also in 1984 a new accounting standard for leases, SSAP 21, resulted in lessees being required to report many leased assets on their own balance sheets for the first time.

By the end of the 1980s around £12.0 billion per year of new asset finance was being arranged (£29bn today).

1990s

Several large banks sold off their leasing operations. G.E. Capital Corporation acquired part of Mercantile Credit in July 1991 from Barclays.

The UK recession of 1990-91 led to a fall in the market of around 10% with a return to normal levels by 1995. By the end of the 1990s around £18 billion per year of new asset finance was being arranged (£30bn today).

2000s

The decade was marked by a dramatic fall of more than 30% in new business between 2008 (£27bn) and 2009 (18.4bn) following the 2008 crisis in the global financial markets. Non-banks were particularly badly hit as some were unable to access any funding, nor the very low cost funds available through the Bank of England to the large banks.

There was a gradual erosion of tax benefits of finance leases due to a combination of the long-funding lease rules, lower corporation tax rates and lower interest rates. This contributed to a decline in big-ticket leasing written in the UK.

2010s

From 2010 to 2016 there was a slow but steady recovery in the market, with volumes back to normal long-term levels of around £30 billion at current prices by the first half of 2016. Leasing also returned to normal investment market share levels of around 30%.

The importance of banks fell slightly reflecting the decline in big-ticket leasing in the UK, non-banks accounting for 22% of total investment in leasing across the market by 2014/15. Within the banking sector, there was particular growth from smaller banks, including Close and Aldermore. The broker and vendor indirect channels also grew and by 2016 accounted together for around 45% of new volume.

A-Z OF TERMS

A   Acceptance certificate

A confirmation signed by the lessee that the assets that will be leased have been received in good condition and are fit for use. Upon receipt by the lessor the lease agreement will usually start.

Use of an acceptance certificate procedure may delay the start of the lease but is a sensible 'stop and check' which can benefit both lessee and lessor. The lessee's risk of being committed to lease payments for equipment which is not yet delivered, not as required or faulty, is reduced. The lessor is less likely to pay a fraudulent supplier or to have to deal with a complaint or default.

An equivalent (or sometimes additional) confirmation may be obtained by phone rather than in writing. Some lessors use a 'deemed acceptance' clause in the lease agreement to place the onus on the lessee to inform them of any problems. Deemed acceptance clauses will usually have a time limit starting at the date of delivery. This means that the lessee will have a set number of days from delivery of the asset to inform the lessor of any problems or the lessee will be deemed to have accepted the asset, triggering the start of the lease agreement.

#Legal #Risk

Acceptance ratio

The proportion of total applications that are accepted following underwriting. Funders will wish to keep the acceptance ratio high, and avoid unnecessary underwriting expense, by providing clear guidance on their lending policies to their direct salesforce and introducers.

It can also be useful to monitor acceptance ratio by introducer, where appropriate. This can help to identify where action is needed either to reduce the level of unacceptable proposals or to review the underwriting policy.

#Credit

Accelerated depreciation

Any method of accounting depreciation that results in a comparatively large expense in the early years of an asset's life and a lower expense in the later years. The Sum of the Digits approach, also known as Rule of 78, which historically was commonly used by UK leasing companies, is an example. Compared to a constant level of depreciation, an accelerated approach leads to lower reported profits in the earlier years of a lease and higher in the later years.

#Accounting

Accounting standards

The rules and guidance for financial reporting that all companies are required to follow when preparing their accounts to be filed at Companies House.

Lease accounting rules in the UK are now contained in Financial Reporting Standards (FRS) issued by the Financial Reporting Council. The FRSs include the core Standard, FRS 102, the simplified FRS 105 for micro-entities (e.g. many companies with turnover below £632,000), and FRS 101 which provides for reduced disclosures for certain subsidiary and other companies. Previously there was a separate standard for leases, Statement of Standard Accounting Practice (SSAP) 21.

Listed companies, banks and insurance companies must follow international accounting standards issued by the International Accounting Standards Board for their consolidated accounts. International Financial Reporting Standard 16 replaced International Accounting Standard 17 for reporting leases in periods ending from January 2019.

#Accounting

Accounting Standards Board

The former name of the regulatory body responsible for setting accounting standards in the UK. The ASB has been subsumed into the Financial Reporting Council.

#Accounting

A   Actuarial method

A method of calculating finance lease interest income for lessor accounting. It is based on the principle that a lessor will earn a constant return on its investment in each period of the lease agreement. The effective interest rate of the lease is therefore used to calculate the interest component of each lease payment. As the lessee repays the principal, the interest earned therefore reduces.

It is considered a more precise way of calculating income than the simpler Rule of 78. The actuarial method usually results in lower interest income in the earlier years of a lease and higher in the later years, but the total for the lease is identical. Auditors would expect the actuarial method to be used unless the difference between the two methods is found not to be material.

The Actuarial rate of return is the percentage margin between the interest income calculated using the actuarial method and the lessor's own cost of finance.

#Accounting

Additions

Often refers to extra features added to leased equipment by the lessee. The lease contract will typically require the lessor to agree to any such modifications, and the additions will become part of the property of the lessor.

The term is also used to refer to lessees adding additional units of equipment to an existing Master lease contract, for example adding extra cars to an existing fleet.

#Contracts

Administration

When a trading entity in financial difficulty enters Administration, a court makes an Administration Order to appoint an Insolvency Practitioner (IP). The order allows for the reorganisation of a company or for it or its assets to be sold. During the administration, which usually lasts for up to 12 months, there is

A

a moratorium on the company's debts. The Company must have the approval of its Creditors to enter an Administration.

The IP will establish the likelihood of the Company being able to trade its way out of difficulty. The IP has powers to make decisions to effect change within the business and its current structure. They take over the responsibilities of the Company's Directors and draw remuneration from the Company's trading receipts.

The administrator must act in the best interests of all creditors, including any lessors. Difficulties can arise when the administrator does not establish that some assets are leased, where the administrator is slow to inform and consult the lessor, or where the administrator does not ensure that leased equipment remains insured and maintained.

#Risk

Advance lease payments

Where the lessee is required to make one or more lease payments in advance of the start of the lease. Such payments may take the form either of a payment in advance (e.g. the first month's rental paid at the inception of the lease), or a security deposit that will then reduce the last payment or payments of the lease. Advance lease payments provide added security to the lessor by reducing their initial exposure.

Advance lease payments are usually separate from any deposit that the lessee will pay to the supplier of equipment that reduces the size of the lease.

#Contracts

Advanced Internal Ratings Based Approach (AIRB)

For prudential regulation, the optional method by which banks calculate their Risk Weighted Assets, an alternative to the Standardised Approach. AIRB risk weightings are an output of risk models developed by banks and approved by the Prudential Regulation Authority.

The AIRB is relatively expensive to set up and run, as it requires large volumes of data. It has the potential to recognise the

A

relatively low risk nature of leasing, which can help banks to offer the most competitive rates for leases. Some banks using AIRB bundle all SME loans together and although the risk weighting will then usually be preferable to that used by banks using the Standardised Approach, it will not recognise the low risk nature of leasing.

The competitive advantage that can be gained by the largest banks has long been a concern for their smaller competitors. The Prudential Regulation Authority has responded by allowing banks without extensive historical data on loan defaults to supplement their own internal data with external market data in calculating credit risk weighted assets. That assists banks in some sectors, but not in leasing where there is no comprehensive sharing of information on default experience.

#Prudential

Advantages of leasing

The benefits of leasing vary dependent upon the type of lease and the lessee's circumstances but will include some combination of the following:

- Lower cost than using retained earnings or bank loans to pay for assets due to:
- Lower Probability of Default on leases compared to bank loans, reducing costs for lessors
- Lower Loss Given Default on leases compared to bank loans, reducing costs for lessors
- Lessee may be eligible to claim tax relief on part or all of the lease payments
- Lessor may be eligible for tax capital allowances when the lessee may not have tax capacity
- The lessor may be able to dispose of assets at lower cost or for higher value
- Availability of 'zero percent' or other 'subsidised' finance from manufacturers.
- Easier to obtain than bank loans:
- Additional source of finance for a business that has limited cash and constrained access to bank loans

- Less need to provide additional security, including liens over business or directors' personal assets
- Less need to review or renegotiate covenants in existing loans or securities.
- Reduces risks compared to using retained earnings or bank loans to pay for assets:
- Asset finance cannot be withdrawn during the term of an agreement
- Lessee may avoid residual value risk on leased assets
- Lessee will avoid interest rate risk if lease payments are fixed not variable.
- Provides additional benefits:
- Helps firms to manage cashflow as lease costs can be broadly aligned with expected income arising from the firm's use of the asset
- Agreement may provide for a replacement to be provided if leased asset requires maintenance or repair
- Special deals for upgrades to newer technology may be available to lessees using captive finance companies or manufacturer-supported vendor finance schemes.

#Alternatives #Market

Affordability

For the FCA's regulation of consumer credit, lessors must specifically assess whether a regulated consumer or business customer will be able to pay for a new lease.

Lessors might consider a range of factors in making their assessment including whether the new agreement will replace an existing lease that the lessee has paid without problems; the size of the agreement relative to the size of the business; a credit agency's report on the business; and a review of the lessee's business, financial position and its plans.

In a review carried out in 2017 and 2018, the FCA noted that using a credit check based on historic information is not enough to assess affordability; it is also necessary to consider the potential for new loans to become unaffordable.

A

Regulated firms should keep records of the basis of their assessments of affordability.

#Conduct

Agency agreement

The contract used where an equipment supplier or manufacturer (the 'agent') enters lease agreements with its customers on behalf and in accordance with the instructions of a lessor (the 'principal').

There are many different types of agency arrangements at law whereby an intermediary agent is involved in contractual dealings between a principal and the principal's customer (see for instance Agency purchase below). However, within leasing, the arrangement described above is one of the most common and significant ones.

The agency arrangement may be disclosed or undisclosed. If the agreement is disclosed, the lessee will be informed that the agent is acting on behalf of a particular lessor. In these scenarios, the lessor will often collect the lease payments. Alternatively, if the agency arrangement is undisclosed, the lessee will not know of the existence of an agent. In these scenarios, the agent will collect the lease payments on behalf of the lessor.

#Legal

Agency purchase

The agency arrangement whereby a lessee is authorised by the lessor to acquire assets on its behalf. In this way the lessee may order equipment from a supplier on the basis that the supplier will invoice the lessor on delivery. It can form part of a wider pre-lease agreement.

#Legal

Agent

For the FCA's regulation of consumer credit, an individual who is appointed by a firm to act as its representative in dealing with customers.

The agent can only work for one firm (the 'principal' firm) and must make clear she/he is representing that firm. For the customer it should make no difference whether the firm's representative is an employee or an agent. The agent does not need their own FCA authorisation as the principal accepts responsibility for the agent's conduct. The principal must ensure its agents are properly supervised with a suitable agreement in place but does not need to register individual agents with the FCA.

Some asset finance brokers appoint agents. Sometimes there may be only one or two agents who are semi-retired or working part-time. Some larger brokers appoint multiple agents to help build their geographical coverage.

Outside of regulated business, the term can refer more generally to any person appointed to represent a lessor.

#Conduct

Aircraft leasing

The largest part of the global equipment leasing market by value, lessors own around one-third of the global aircraft fleet.

The largest lessors include GE Capital Aviation Services with over 2,000 leased aircraft, Aercap with 1,250 aircraft, CIT, and SMBC Aviation Capital (formerly RBS Aviation Capital) with 440 aircraft. At the time of publication, CIT was being purchased by Avalon Holdings of China.

The sector comes with its own distinct terminology. In a dry lease the aircraft are operated by the lessee. In a wet lease they are operated by the lessor who is an airline itself. A damp (sometimes called 'moist') lease is a wet lease that comes without the cabin crew.

Dublin is a major global centre for the aviation leasing industry, partly because of Ireland's low rate of corporation tax but increasingly reflecting the expertise in place there. It is estimated that around half of the world's leased aircraft pool of 7,000 aircraft are leased through Ireland, with an estimated value of more than $100 billion.

#Market

A   Alternative finance

Finance that is 'non-conventional' as it is provided from outside of the banking system. It includes crowdfunding, peer-to-peer lending, and invoice trading where businesses sell their invoices through an online marketplace. Leasing is probably too well-established to be classified by most people as alternative finance, despite the leasing market being the largest provider of non-bank business debt finance.

#Alternatives

Amortisation

For lease accounting, an accounting estimate of the reduction in the value of a lease as lease payments are made over time. A lease is said to be fully amortised once the whole of the original capital value less any residual value has been repaid with interest. It is calculated using the Effective interest method.

The amortised cost is the amount at which the lease is valued by the lessor. It comprises the initial amount recognised, minus the cumulative amortisation, adjusted for any loss allowance.

#Accounting

Annual Investment Allowance (AIA)

Tax rules allowing companies to deduct the full value of qualifying assets from their profit before tax in the year they buy it. From 2016 businesses may deduct up to £200,000 per year. AIAs only bring forward capital allowances from later years, they do not increase the overall tax deductions available when investing in assets.

Lessees eligible to claim capital allowances, including for hire purchase agreements, can benefit from the AIA if they have sufficient taxable profits to offset. AIAs are not available for cars. They are also not useful where the lessor is eligible for capital allowances.

#Tax

Annualised Percentage Rate (APR)

The annual rate of interest on a credit agreement. For regulated consumer credit, the APR is calculated in a standard way to include all costs which the borrower will pay under the terms of the agreement. These include interest, fees and any other charges, whether payable to the lender or to anyone else. The APR is based on the amortised value of the lease, so it is usually at least double the flat rate.

There are complex rules in the Consumer Credit Act on how APRs may be used in marketing. For example, advertisements that feature interest rates must show a 'Representative APR' that at least 51% of the customers for credit agreements expected to be made will pay.

#Conduct

Annual service fee

Some lessors charge lessees an annual fee in addition to their regular lease payments. For consumer credit regulated agreements, this fee should be included in the Annualised Percentage Rate calculation. Some in the industry argue that the fee is unjustified, while others point to the ongoing need to monitor the contract and asset risk.

#Contracts

Anti-Money Laundering (AML)

Steps to prevent the financial system being used to facilitate crime and terrorism. Lessors and their brokers and introducers need to check they are dealing with representatives of genuine businesses.

Some factors indicate that leasing is a low risk activity for money laundering. Funds are not released to the lessee but rather to the equipment supplier, payments are usually collected from pre-existing UK bank accounts using direct debits, and cash payments are not normally accepted.

On the other hand, leasing could be a low-cost way of obtaining assets to be used in criminal or terrorist activities.

A   Early settlement of agreements could also potentially be a way of distributing illegally obtained money.

Both the FCA and the Joint Money Laundering Steering Group publish guidance on AML checks. All lessors need to register with an AML supervisor, usually the FCA, and should have a designated Money Laundering Reporting Officer (MLRO).

#Regulation

Appointed Representative (AR)

For FCA consumer credit regulation, a firm or individual who carries out regulated activities on behalf of a firm that is directly authorised by the FCA (the 'principal' firm). The AR is not then directly authorised by the FCA.

The AR must inform a regulated customer that it is acting as an AR of the principal firm but it can trade under a different name. The principal must have an agreement with the AR, must register the AR with the FCA and is responsible for checking the AR meets the FCA's requirements.

A variant of AR is Introducer Appointed Representative (IAR). An IAR may only introduce a regulated customer to the principal firm, it cannot discuss or otherwise get involved in the customer's financial needs. The IAR is therefore generally seen as less risky for the principal than an AR.

Some asset finance brokers appoint other smaller brokers as their ARs and dealers as either ARs or IARs. Few lessors have chosen to take on the responsibility for supervising other firms in this way.

#Conduct #Intermediaries

Appraisal

An expert report on the current and expected future value of an asset, likely to be based on an inspection and knowledge of the second-hand market. It is generally used by lessors for higher value assets such as aircraft. Due to the cost, lessors tend to rely on their own checks and asset expertise, or that of trusted specialist brokers, for most types of equipment.

#Assets

Arrears

Money owed by the lessee to the lessor that should already have been paid. Arrears may be caused by a failed direct debit payment due to lack of funds or a payment stopped by the customer. There might also be technical errors in setting up or amending direct debit arrangements.

Average arrears levels across the industry are typically between 1% and 2% of the value of lessors' books.

Separately, the term can also refer to an option for how lease payments are made. Instead of payment being required 'in advance' at the beginning of each period, it may be due 'in arrears' at the end of each period.

#Credit

Artificial Intelligence (AI)

The use of software algorithms that are learning how to solve problems previously only associated with human decision-making. The predicted impacts of AI are so great that it is often called the 'Fourth Industrial Revolution' and AI is now being used in many applications in financial services. AI may have less impact when there are smaller numbers of transactions, such as in asset finance.

Accounting firms have claimed they can use AI to extract key information from large numbers of lease contracts that is needed to prepare accounts to meet IFRS 16 requirements. There could be many more emerging applications.

#Operations

Asset

Items of plant, property and equipment that might be leased. In general, plant is immovable and equipment is movable, although in some circumstances equipment may be treated as fixed to a building for legal and tax purposes. In addition to these tangible items, some intangible assets such as software licences might also

A

be leased. Assets may also be categorised as Hard assets or Soft assets for leasing purposes.

#Asset

Asset-Backed Commercial Paper (ABCP)

Short-term debt securities backed by assets from multiple sellers that may include asset finance portfolios. ABCP is issued by a conduit, or structured investment vehicle, usually set up by a sponsoring bank. ABCP is used by lessors in the United States and Canada but lessors in Europe generally issue Asset-Backed Securities.

#Funding

Asset-Backed Securities (ABS)

Debt securities that may be issued by lessors, most commonly by captive car lessors.

The lessor's payments to the investors in the debt are backed by rights to portfolios of lease agreements and the assets underlying those agreements. The portfolio of leases may be placed in a special purpose vehicle (SPV). In the event of the lessor not being able to pay the investors, the income from the leases would then be paid directly from the SPV to the investors.

Some ABS issued by lessors in Europe is raised without the use of an SPV. This approach helps to manage the debt issuance costs. The investors would still have rights to a portfolio of leases that can change over time. The security of the assets is supported by guarantees from a captive's parent company, or a bank or another sponsor. Many issues have also been supported by the European Investment Fund.

#Funding

Asset Based Finance Association (ABFA)

The trade association representing the factoring, invoice discounting and asset-based lending finance industries in the UK and Ireland. Originally founded in 1976 as the Association of British Factors, it took on its current name in 2007. In 2015, members of the ABFA provided around £20 billion of funding **A** to 44,000 British and Irish businesses.

The Association operates a code of conduct for its members and an independent complaints mediation service, both of which are overseen by an independent Professional Standards Council. ABFA has become part of the new consolidated trade association for the financial services industry (see UK Finance).

#Associations

Asset based finance

Business lending secured against business assets, usually invoices issued by the business but not yet paid. Lending secured against invoices is termed factoring if it includes debt management and collection services, or invoice discounting if not. Less routinely other assets may also be used as collateral for loans, termed Asset-Based Lending (ABL). Unlike leasing, the lender does not own the assets but instead has liens over them.

#Alternatives

Asset disposal

The process by which lessors deal with equipment that is returned to them at end of lease. It may be sold, leased to a different customer, recycled or scrapped.

The lease agreement might specify that the lessee will dispose of it on behalf of the lessor. In that case the lessee might be entitled to keep most of the proceeds of the sale. This can provide an extra incentive for the lessee to keep the asset in good condition.

The lessor might have an arrangement with a broker or equipment supplier to take back the equipment. If equipment does come back to the lessor, it can be sold, offered on a lease to a new customer, disposed of for scrap or recycled.

Lessors can have some responsibility under data protection law to ensure that any confidential data has been removed from relevant asset types. The Asset Disposal and Information Security Alliance issues guidance on good practice in meeting this responsibility.

A

What might once have been seen as a relatively unimportant part of the leasing value chain is now becoming a key point of competitive advantage and differentiation. As part of the trend towards the 'circular economy' lessees increasingly want to know that their returned equipment will be dealt with in the most environmentally-friendly way possible.

#Assets

Asset finance

Any business credit or hire arrangements where the lender or hirer owns the equipment during the period of the credit or hire period. Includes finance lease, operating lease, hire purchase, contract hire and other products. Virtually synonymous with the term 'leasing' except that leasing would also cover property. A hire agreement of up to one year would generally be considered a rental product and not asset finance.

#Market

Asset Finance 50

Ranking survey of UK lessors, first published in 2016 by Asset Finance Policy and Asset Finance International. The tables show lessors' net investment in business equipment leasing based on their published accounts. The 2018 edition shows that the top ten firms account for around 58% of the market (up from 54% in 2016). Banks accounted for two-thirds of the market.

The key results are shown at the back of this book and the full survey is available to download from the Asset Finance International website.
www.assetfinanceinternational.com

#Market

Asset Finance 500

Website that aims to list all leasing brokers in the UK that have websites, published by Asset Finance Policy. Around 650 firms

are listed by region, helping small businesses to find a suitable local asset finance expert.
www.assetfinance500.uk

#Market

Asset Finance International

Online industry news website based in the UK but with sections covering Europe, Asia and the Americas. It offers free access to industry professionals. In addition to daily news updates it publishes many special reports, including the Asset Finance Pricing Review for the fleet market, country surveys, technology research, and the Asset Finance 50 industry ranking survey.
www.assetfinanceinternational.com

#Market

Asset Finance Professionals Association (AF-PA)

A forum for professionals from the asset finance industry to network informally and to raise funds for member nominated charities. A registered charity (AFPA Trust), it holds bi-annual receptions in London and various other events. Through its wider network, it aims to help anyone in the industry to realise their personal and professional goals and also seeks to promote the highest professional standards.
www.af-pa.org

#Associations

Asset register

To help prevent theft, fraud including double financing, and to help protect assets if a lessee becomes insolvent or enters administration, lessors may wish to record their ownership of assets on a publicly available register.

Any on-road vehicle has a Vehicle Identification Number (VIN) and lessors will register their financial interest against this on a database operated by HPI Limited, a subsidiary of the American company Solera Holdings.

Other assets may also be registered on HPI using serial

A

numbers. Unlike with VINs the HPI system cannot verify the serial number against the type of asset. Accuracy in recording and checking numbers is therefore essential.

For many years the legal profession has been exploring ways in which lessors and others could register their interest in assets at Companies House, but this has not yet proven feasible.

Many serial number labels on assets are easy for fraudsters to alter or replace. The Construction & Agricultural Equipment Security and Registration Scheme (CESAR) is designed to overcome this problem for plant and machinery.

#Assets #Risk

Assignment

The transfer of legal rights from one person (the 'assignor') to another (the 'assignee').

A lessee might transfer its rights to use the asset or a lessor might transfer its rights to receive rentals for the remaining lease term. Technically, at law, only the 'benefit' of a contract can be assigned (i.e. the lessee's right to use an asset or the lessor's right to receive rentals). The 'burden' of a contract cannot be assigned (i.e. the lessee's obligation to pay rentals or the lessor's general obligations under the contract). This means that the assignor will remain liable for the burden of the contract event after the assignment has taken place. In practice, however, the assignee will usually assume performance of the contract and indemnify the assignor for liability arising after the assignment has taken place.

Lease agreements will typically require the lessee to obtain the lessor's consent. This is because, apart from keeping good records, the lessor will be concerned that the assignment could increase the risk of default.

Assignments can either be disclosed or undisclosed. This will be determined by whether a notice of assignment has been served on the other party to the contract (that is, if notice has been served, the assignment will be disclosed, and if notice has not been served, the assignment will be undisclosed). Disclosure is important as it may determine what type of assignment it is. 'Legal assignments' allow the assignee to enforce the assigned rights themselves. 'Equitable assignments' require the assignee to rely on the assignor to enforce the assigned rights. One of the requirements for a legal assignment is disclosure/notice of assignment.

There may, however, exist compelling reasons not to disclose the assignment and to have only an equitable assignment. Choosing to do so will, however, carry an increased risk to the assignee as they will need to rely on the assignor.

If there are valid reasons for a lease to be transferred away from a lessee, for example the lessee is acquired, the lessor will normally prefer to novate the lease to the new party (see Novation). This is because it avoids the potential technical complications set out in this section.

Other reasons why a lessor may want to transfer lease agreements include situations where a lessor's book is in run-off, or if a lessor places a portfolio of leases in a special purpose vehicle as part of a securitisation.

#Legal

Audit

The formal inspection of accounts by a qualified external accountant. As part of the audit report, the auditor is legally obliged, under Companies Act 2006, to provide an opinion on whether the accounts give a true and fair view of the company's affairs. Most UK companies are now exempt from the need to have their accounts audited. This has redu ced the reliance that lessors can place on company accounts.

The involvement of an external professional accountant, usually a member of one of the chartered accountancy bodies registered as a 'member in practice', may still provide a degree of assurance over the accuracy of the accounts although the scope of the work carried out can vary significantly.

The demise of the audit has also led to greater financial pressures on some small audit firms.

#Accounting #Risk

Back to back lease

B

Where assets are leased to another lessor and then subleased on the same terms to the end-lessee. More common in the property leasing market. See Head lessor.

#Products

Bad debt

Amounts owed to a lessor that are no longer expected to be paid. They are written-off as losses for accounting purposes. A more common term used in the industry is default.

#Credit #Risk

Bailment

The temporary transfer of assets from one person to another, bailment is the legal concept that sits behind leases for which there is no purchase option. Ownership of the asset remains with the lessor. Under the Supply of Goods and Services Act 1982 the lessor cannot disturb the lessee's 'quiet possession' of the leased asset provided the terms of the agreement are being met.

#Legal

Balance sheet

Financial statement showing the financial position of a business at a specific point in time. The statement will show the firm's assets, liabilities and shareholders' funds. Under current accounting rules the lessee's balance sheet will list assets leased using finance leases but not operating leases. Under IFRS 16, it will include all leased assets.

#Accounting

Balloon payment

A final payment for an asset finance agreement that is larger than the previous monthly or other periodic payments. Often referred to simply as a balloon. It is most commonly found on hire purchase contracts, for which ownership of the asset will transfer to the lessee only after payment of the balloon. The size of the balloon is set when the lease is entered into and is not linked to the residual value of the asset.

Lessees need to understand their obligation to pay the balloon. When comparing lease options, lessees also need to consider the overall cost of the lease, not only the regular payments.

#Contracts

Bank lessor

A deposit-taking bank that is a lessor itself or a leasing subsidiary of a bank. Seven of the largest UK lessors are banks. The largest bank lessors, according to the Asset Finance 50, are Royal Bank of Scotland (including its subsidiary, Lombard), Barclays, HSBC, Lloyds, Santander, Close and Aldermore.

#Market

Bank of England

The UK's Central Bank. The Prudential Regulation Authority (PRA) is part of the Bank. The BoE carries out market operations in which it buys aims to boost lending in the economy. At present, for example, this is done through the Funding for Lending Scheme Extension and the new Term Funding Scheme.
www.bankofengland.co.uk

#Bodies

Bank of International Settlements (BIS)

The body that facilitates collaboration between national central banks.

Established in 1930 and based in Basel, Switzerland, the BIS has 60 central bank members from around the world. Its mission is to serve central banks in their pursuit of monetary and financial stability, to foster international cooperation in those areas and to act as a bank for central banks.

The BIS's Basel Committee on Banking Supervision sets standards for the Prudential regulation and supervision of

B

banks which are then implemented by the Bank of England in the UK and the European Central Bank for the Eurozone. Although individual central banks have some flexibility in implementation, the prudential treatment of leasing rests largely on the Committee's work.

www.bis.org

#Bodies #Prudential

Bank Referral Scheme

Under the Bank Referral Scheme, large UK banks are obliged to offer small businesses whose applications for finance leases (and other types of loans) are rejected a referral to a designated online platform that may be able to help find alternative sources of finance. The alternative platforms available each include asset finance funders. The Scheme is overseen by the British Business Bank and was launched in 2016 The government policy aims to address the 'funding gap' caused by declined applications for finance. Take-up in the first two years was low but it is growing.

#Regulation

Bankruptcy

The process by which an individual, who may or may not be in business, is declared insolvent by a Court. The individual's assets, with certain exceptions, are converted into money and distributed among their creditors to satisfy debt. Creditors are unable to pursue parties that have been made bankrupt.

#Risk

Bargain purchase option

The opportunity for the lessee to purchase a leased asset at the end of the lease term at a price that is significantly below the asset's market value.

Given the low price many lessees can be expected to take up the option. Many hire purchase agreements include bargain purchase options, also commonly called Option to purchase. For tax purposes only those agreements that have bargain purchase options are classified as hire purchase agreements.

#Contracts

B

Bargain renewal option

The opportunity for the lessee to extend the lease at the end of the lease term at a rate significantly below the normal market level. This could be a Peppercorn rate. Given the low cost many lessees can be expected to take up the option. The term is used for lease accounting and is not otherwise in common use.

#Accounting #Contracts

Basel Committee

See Bank of International Settlements.

#Bodies #Prudential

Basis point

An interest rate difference of one-hundredth of a percentage point. The Spread is often expressed in basis points. For example, a spread of 3% is 300 basis points.

#Finance

BEN

The Motor and Allied Trades Benevolent Fund, a not-for-profit organisation, dedicated to those who work, or have worked, in the automotive industry and their family dependents. BEN offers practical help, support and advice, and it operates highly-regarded care centres. It is supported by many organisations in the vehicle leasing market.

#Market

Big data analytics

The process of analysing large amounts of data from multiple sources. Advances in software and database technology have

B

made big data analytics much easier to deploy, and some leasing companies and (more often) their service providers, are beginning to exploit it. Examples include credit agencies using data about businesses and their directors integrated from a range of sources, and lessors' risk management teams forecasting future defaults and losses.

#Operations

Big-ticket lease

Leasing of high-value assets such as aircraft, ships and trains. The FLA refers to 'high value' leases which are for projects over £20 million, the ELFA to financings over $5 million. Such agreements typically involve specialist legal and tax expertise.

Big-ticket leasing in the UK has declined greatly with the demise of major tax incentives. In 2002 it represented 25% of new leasing by value and by 2015 it was just 3%. The recent statistics may understate the importance of the sector, however, as many big-ticket leases are still planned and sold in the UK even if the lease agreement is written elsewhere.

#Market

Bill of Sale

A document that transfers ownership of goods from one person (A) to another in circumstances where A retains possession of the goods.

Bills of Sale are also a way in which individuals can use goods they already own as security for a loan or other obligations, while retaining possession of those goods – like taking a mortgage in respect of the goods. The Bill of Sale allows a lender to seize assets without a court order on default. Those for motor vehicles include so-called 'logbook loans'. For some assets, such as high-value cars or works of art, they can be used as alternatives to leases.

Taking security by way of Bill of Sales is complex as they are governed by statutes dating from 1878 and 1882. In September 2014, the government asked the Law Commission to review the Bills of Sale Acts and make recommendations for its reform. The Commission recommended that the Acts should be repealed and replaced with a new "Goods Mortgages Act" and whilst this recommendation formed part of the Queen's speech in 2017, the government decided in May 2018 that it would not introduce legislation at this point in time, citing a small and reducing market and the wider work on high-cost credit. Similar attempts at bringing the relevant legislation into the 21st century in Scotland have also been defeated where the Scottish Parliament announced in September 2018 that the Moveable Transactions (Scotland) Bill would not form part of the legislative agenda for 2018/2019

#Alternatives

Blind discount

An arrangement whereby an equipment manufacturer or supplier subsidises the cost of equipment to be leased, without the customer being made aware of this. The subsidy reduces the price actually paid for the asset by the leasing company. This can enable the lessor to offer a low or Zero percent deal to the customer. Care is needed for regulated agreements to ensure compliance with APR regulations.

#Market

Blockchain

An electronic register that is shared between at least three users, and often many more. Each copy of the register shows the same information. The register is secure, and transactions cannot be changed once recorded. All parties must agree before a new transaction is added.

Many see potential for use of blockchain in leasing. Blockchain might, for example, expedite the preparation of Big-ticket lease agreements that may involve many different parties (e.g. lawyers, accountants, tax specialists and maintenance companies in addition to the lessee and lessor themselves).

#Market

Block discounting

B

Where a lessor 'sells' the rights to multiple finance agreements to a larger finance company, usually a specialist division of that company. The portfolio being sold will be to an agreed maximum value and for agreements meeting agreed criteria.

The purchaser will usually insist that the seller keeps an interest in all agreements. The arrangement is usually undisclosed to the customers as all dealings with the customer – including the work to 'bill and collect' payments' – will continue to be the responsibility of the seller. The technique is used by smaller lessors including brokers wishing to grow their own-book without having to introduce all the normally required capital themselves.

#Funding

Book value

The value at which an asset is reported (or 'carried') on a balance sheet. For operating leases, assets are initially shown on the balance sheet of the lessor at cost price when purchased. The book value is then calculated as cost minus accumulated depreciation, plus or minus any adjustments that might be needed due to revaluations.

#Accounting

Bond

A debt security that obligates the issuer to pay the security's face value amount on a specified future date in addition to interest payments. Bonds are commonly used by large lessors, mainly in the US and Far East, to raise capital for lending. They are also used by lessors in some European countries, including Germany and Italy.

#Funding

Break option

Where a lease agreement allows the lessee to cancel the agreement on certain dates (the 'breakdate'), at a pre-defined cost. Few lease agreements include such clauses.

#Contracts

British Bankers' Association (BBA)

Until 2017, the association of banks based in, or with branches in, the UK. The BBA merged with other trade associations to form UK Finance.

#Associations

British Business Bank (BBB)

UK government-owned institution that aims to make finance markets work better for small and medium-sized businesses (SMEs).

It launched in 2014 with an initial £1 billion of government funding. It runs a variety of schemes and programmes, including some previously operated by the Department for Business and its subsidiary Capital for Enterprise Limited.

The BBB is not an authorised banking institution and hence all its operations work through finance company partners including a range of lessors. Non-bank lessors may borrow from the BBB. Lessors may also obtain a Government-backed portfolio guarantee in return for a fee. The Enterprise Finance Guarantee, which provides guarantees for individual loans, is also being extended to cover leasing.

www.british-business-bank.co.uk

#Bodies

British Vehicle Rental and Leasing Association (BVRLA)

The trade body for companies engaged in the rental and leasing of cars and commercial vehicles. Established in 1967, it has around 500 member companies. BVRLA members own 2.5 million cars,

vans and trucks. The BVRLA promotes the interests of the sector, has a code of conduct and operates a conciliation service for its members and their customers to help resolve disputes.
www.bvrla.co.uk

#Associations

Broker

An intermediary who arranges transactions between lessees and lessors. There are at least 750 asset finance brokers in the UK. The majority are listed on the Asset Finance 500 website. Finance brokers earn commission from lessors. Most are now regulated by the Financial Conduct Authority to permit the broking of regulated agreements.

 # Intermediaries

Business Debtline

Run by the Charity Money Advice Trust, offering free online debt advice for the self-employed and small businesses. It has a fact sheet on hire purchase and conditional sale and helps businesses to apply for Time orders to reschedule payments or to terminate agreements. Another charity, StepChange, provides similar services to individual consumers.
www.businessdebtline.org

#Credit

Business risk

The uncertainty faced by a business due to factors specific to its own business, such as changes in the marketplace, reduced sales or profitability. Part of the overall assessment of the risk of lending.

#Risk

Buy-back

Where a lessor arranges with the supplier to buy back the assets at the end of the lease. Some captive finance companies have a buy-back arrangement with their parent manufacturers. The technique is also used by vendor finance specialist lessors working with very well-established equipment manufacturers. A risk to the lessor is that the supplier ceases trading during the period of the lease.

#Assets

Call option

Where an equipment supplier has the right to buy back the equipment it sold to a lessor for use by a particular lessee at a specified price. The option would typically be available at the end of the lease agreement or in the event of the equipment being repossessed following a default. Not a common arrangement.

#Assets

Capital adequacy

The minimum amount of capital that banks are required to hold in proportion to their risk-adjusted assets.

The rules distinguish between 'tier one' and 'tier two' capital. Tier one is core capital that is relatively transparent and secure, including equity and reserves. Tier two capital is less reliable capital, including categories such as revaluation reserves. Under Basel III rules, banks must have tier one capital equivalent to at least 7 percent of their risk-weighted assets (RWAs) and minimum total capital of 10.5 percent of RWAs. The largest, 'global systemically important banks', will have further capital adequacy rules from 2019.

RWAs reflect the value of assets, the Probability of default (PD), and the expected Loss given default (LGD) for different asset categories. Banks can either adopt 'standardised' risk weightings that are issued by the Prudential Regulation Authority based on the Capital Requirement Directive, or may use internal models of risk if approved by the PRA.

Leaseurope research has shown that leasing is much lower risk than other types of lending to businesses. The standardised approach does not distinguish between different types of small business lending, although there is a lower risk weighting for all 'retail' (including small business) exposures.

A lessor able to demonstrate that leasing is very low risk through an approved internal model can benefit from holding less capital than a competitor using the standardised risk weightings, reducing its cost of funding for leasing business. This does require very strong data sets. Few banks do, in practice, distinguish between different leasing and other SME lending products in their capital adequacy models. For this reason, the key effect of the capital adequacy regime tends to be on competition between lessors, rather than competition between leasing and alternative financial products.

#Prudential

Capital allowances

The amount of depreciation that can be offset against taxable profits, reducing the amount of tax paid. Commercially calculated depreciation is not allowable for tax but instead of this tax has its own system of writing down assets by capital allowances generally given annually with a balancing allowance or charge when the asset is disposed of. The tax rules are complicated but for hire purchase and most finance leases the lessee claims the capital allowances and for most operating leases it is the lessor.

The allowances are calculated as a percentage of the initial cost of the equipment or the written-down value at the end of the previous tax year. Special (higher) rates apply to some investments including Enhanced Capital Allowances and First Year Capital Allowances.

#Tax

Capital charges

A now defunct public sector accounting term but one that still helps explain attitudes to leasing in the public sector.

Public sector bodies used to use cash accounting techniques and did not maintain balance sheets. This led to concerns that National Health Service hospital trusts and other bodies were not managing their assets efficiently. To address this, the capital charge was introduced in the NHS from 1992 and extended across the public sector from 2000. The charge was a proxy for the cost of capital spent on assets and asset depreciation. It was applied to leased as well as owned assets, arguably overstating the true cost of leasing.

NHS Trusts and other parts of the public sector now use balance sheets and report depreciation rather than the capital charge.

#Public sector

Capital employed

Sum of all money tied up in a business, including fixed assets and working capital.

#Accounting

Capital expenditure

Investment in fixed assets by a company. A key benefit of leasing is the ability to obtain use of assets without incurring the up-front capital expenditure. Capital-intensive businesses require large investments in capital assets, and therefore high capital expenditure, if leasing is not used.

#Accounting

Capital markets

The markets in which businesses can raise debt and equity finance.

#Funding

Capitalised value

For lease accounting, leases are 'capitalised', or reported as an asset at Book value, by either the lessee or the lessor. Under IAS 17 and UK Financial Reporting Standards, at the start of a lease the lessee capitalises the present value of the future lease payments for finance leases. The lessor capitalises the cost of the assets included in the lease, together with any qualifying expenses, for operating leases. Under IFRS 16, the lessee capitalises the present value of the future lease payments for all leases. Lessor accounting is unchanged, thus both the lessee and the lessor will capitalise operating leases.

#Accounting

C

Captive lessor

A lessor whose principal purpose is to provide leasing facilities for the products of the related manufacturer or supplier. May be a subsidiary of the manufacturer or a joint venture with a leasing company or bank. It may lend using its manufacturer parent's own funds or may raise funds in the capital markets.

#Market

Captives forum

Grouping of captive finance companies that seeks to promote the best possible trading conditions for captives across Europe. The Forum is managed by an executive committee of leaders of captives and holds quarterly meetings.
www.captivesforum.org

#Associations

Carry forward

The ability to defer tax allowances, including capital allowances and loss reliefs, from one year to another. From 2015 there has been a restriction on the proportion of banks' annual taxable profit that can be offset by carried forward losses.

#Tax

Cashflow

The actual inflows and outflows of cash faced by a business. A key benefit of leasing is in helping businesses to manage their cashflow whilst obtaining the use of assets critical to their success. Part of lessors' credit analysis process is to establish that a business can afford lease payments, based not only on their accounting profitability but also their ability to find the cash to make the lease payments. A cashflow forecast might be requested from the business for this purpose.

#Credit #Finance

Chartered Institute of Credit Management (CICM)

The main professional body for the credit community, granted the Royal Charter in 2014. It trains and offers qualifications for professionals working in credit and collections functions mainly in non-financial businesses. Many decision makers or decision influencers in companies using or considering leasing are CICM members. It has published a guide to leasing with the FLA and NACFB, 'Investing in equipment', which explains the benefits as well as some possible risks of leasing.
www.cicm.com

#Bodies

Chattel mortgage

A fixed-term loan for the acquisition of, and secured against, an item of property other than land. The customer owns the asset from the start and pays regular periodic payments for the duration of the agreement. Like a hire purchase, there may be an option of reducing the regular payments using a final balloon payment.

#Alternatives

CIFAS

The UK's fraud prevention service for the financial services industry. Its mission is to deter, detect and prevent fraud and related financial crime. CIFAS runs a database of confirmed fraud cases. The database helps lessors to identify connections with current customers or new applications. CIFAS members can access the database directly. The credit reference agencies also reflect CIFAS cases in their credit reports. Information on suspected fraud cases in the leasing industry is shared separately, see D&B.
www.cifas.org.uk

#Risk

Circular economy

C

The antidote to modern society's 'take, make and dispose' economic model. It is an economy in which assets are designed to be repaired, reused or recycled, not disposed of.

Leasing can be an enabler of the circular economy. Lessors can promote leasing of equipment that is likely to retain its value, find new customers for refurbished off-lease equipment, and may work with manufacturers to facilitate the remanufacture, or recycling of obsolete equipment.

It has even been suggested by a Member of the European Parliament that manufacturers should be obliged to lease rather than sell all their equipment, to incentivise them to make their products more durable and sustainable. The EC has adopted a Circular Economy Strategy.

#Market

Claims Management Company (CMC)

A company that offers a service for people or firms seeking to claim compensation, including for mis-sold financial products and services. CMCs have been particularly prominent in relation to PPI mis-selling. A few CMCs have also tried to sell their services to lessees, including schools that might have Ultra vires leases (i.e. leases entered into without requisite authority). In general, they have had limited success, but they can still lead to considerable cost and disruption for lessors.

#Risk

Clawbacks

Where a leasing broker is obliged to repay some or all its commission to the lessor in certain circumstances, for example if the lease agreement goes into default.

#Intermediaries

Club loan

A loan from a small syndicate of banks. Non-bank lessors might raise finance using a club loan facility although it is unusual.

#Funding

C

Collateral risk

For lessors, the risk that where additional collateral is taken, for example directors' guarantees or Liens against personal or business assets, it will prove to be less valuable than expected if it has to be called upon.

For funding, where a lessor issues Asset-backed securities, the risk to investors that the cashflows from the underlying portfolio of leases will not materialise or will fall short of the amounts required.

#Funding #Risk

Collaterised lease equipment obligations

An American term for asset-backed securities where receivables from portfolios of equipment assets provide the security.

#Funding

Collections

Usually refers to the activities of a specialist team in handling lease agreements in arrears, either internal to the lessor or to an external debt collection agency. The referral of lease contracts to a collections team should achieve the joint objectives of helping to recover the debt and ensuring compliance with the detailed FCA rules affecting regulated agreements.

#Credit

Commercial CAIS

A database run by Experian that shows smaller businesses' track record in paying for their credit agreements. Finance companies, including many lessors, supply information on their customers and may access the information provided by other members. Information shared includes the start date and length of the agreement, credit outstanding and whether payments have been made on time.

The data is shared with other credit reference agencies under arrangements overseen by a cross industry group, the Steering Committee on Reciprocity (SCOR). The lessee's agreement is required before their records can be shared. The parallel CAIS system holds information on individuals' credit agreements.

#Credit

Commissions

Cash payments or other rewards paid by lessors to brokers, suppliers or any other intermediaries. The standard commission structure for leasing is a 'Difference in Charges' model, where the lessor quotes the rate it is willing to offer finance at, and the broker adds a commission margin to this. The model can be perceived as rewarding brokers for charging higher rates. The competitive nature of the market; commission caps set by some lessors; and brokers' own policies help to ensure that lessees do not pay excessive rates.

Some lessors are, however, moving away from the Difference in Charges model particularly when working with car dealers, instead setting both the rates that customers will pay and commission levels.

#Intermediaries

Commitment letter

Document which confirms a lessee's intention to enter into a lease, and which is drawn up before the lease agreement is signed. It sets out the headline terms of the proposed lease agreement. It is used for large transactions, such as aircraft leases, where the lessor might be required to incur expenses before the full details of the lease are ready to agree. It can be stated that it is not legally binding, but in general the lessee would be liable to pay damages if they chose to walk away, i.e. not agree or sign the proposed lease agreement.

A commitment fee may be payable at the time the lessee signs the letter. This is akin to a deposit.

#Contracts

Common law

The legal system governing England and Wales, a system characterised by judicial precedents of cases processed by courts who interpret legislation (e.g. acts of Parliament, or international laws). Common law establishes, for example, that a lease with no transfer of ownership of the assets is a contract of bailment, and a lease agreement may be illegal if the assets are to be used for illegal purposes.

#Legal

Conditional sale

A lease that is a credit agreement in legal terms (not hire) as ownership of the asset transfers automatically to the lessee at the end of the term, if the lessee has met all the conditions. Unlike hire purchase, transfer of ownership is not reliant on an option to purchase being exercised.

#Products

Conduct of business

For consumer credit regulated business, the Consumer Credit Sourcebook (CONC) section of the FCA Handbook. There are rules covering financial promotions, pre-contractual requirements, responsible lending, arrears, defaults and recovery. Some rules apply only to credit, others to hire and credit. Some apply to all regulated firms, others to either brokers, hirers or lenders.

#Conduct

Construction & Agricultural Equipment Security and Registration Scheme (CESAR)

C

A secure labelling system for plant and machinery, backed by the Construction Equipment Association and the Agricultural Engineers Association and operated by Datatag.

Many farm and construction equipment manufacturers fit CESAR identification during the production process. In addition to visible tamper-proof identification plates the system encompasses hidden transponders and DNA labelling.

The scheme aims to cut theft of construction plant and agricultural machinery by reducing reliance on traditional registration or serial number plates which are relatively easy to alter. Lessors can register their ownership of equipment fitted with CESAR plates on HPI allowing their interest to be seen in provenance checks by other finance companies and the police. *www.cesarscheme.org*

#Risk

Consumables

The often mundane items that are needed when using leased assets such as toner for printers. For convenience, some leases may come bundled with a supply of consumables. The lessee needs to be confident that the quantities being supplied are suitable, the arrangement will represent good value for its duration, and the period of the supply of consumables is no longer than the term of the lease.

There have been incidents where consumables have been offered to a customer free of charge by a supplier, either on an undocumented basis or through a side-letter. This can be risky for both lessee and lessor as the supplier may not provide the consumables.

#Contracts #Risk

Consumer credit

Lease agreements regulated under the UK's Consumer Credit Act and the Financial Services and Markets Act. The regulator for consumer credit is the Financial Conduct Authority (FCA). Most credit or hire products, including all leasing, are regulated when provided to individuals, unincorporated businesses or unincorporated partnerships of 2 or 3 partners. A wide range of activities involved in consumer credit are regulated, including broking and dealing with the debts of regulated customers.

Most of the asset finance market is not regulated for consumer credit purposes. Around 70% of small businesses are companies and are not regulated and that proportion has been growing in recent years. Only 5% of asset finance business users are likely to be FCA-regulated and around 2% of the market by value. The regulation is, however, particularly important in agricultural equipment leasing and in professions such as design and architecture, where many firms are unincorporated.

Although only a small part of the market, any lessors or intermediaries wishing to serve regulated customers must register with the FCA and comply with its Rulebook. Some of the FCA's rules apply across the business, not only when dealing with regulated customers.

#Conduct

Consumer Credit Act

Legislation that governs agreements with unincorporated bodies where the transaction is non-exempt. Exemptions may apply to agreements over £25,000 for business use and to high net worth individuals. Some parts of the Act have been incorporated into the FCA's Handbook and have been repealed but other parts (the 'retained provisions') remain in place.

#Conduct

Consumer Credit Sourcebook (CONC)

See Conduct of Business.

#Conduct

Consumer Credit Trade Association (CCTA)

C

Founded in 1891, the CCTA is the trade organisation for firms specialising in consumer lending. It started life as the Hire Traders Protection Association, became the Hire Purchase Trade Association in 1949, and then the CCTA in 1978. Many smaller lessors including brokers with own-books join the CCTA to obtain practical support with their consumer credit activities including access to model credit agreements that are compliant with the relevant legislation.
www.ccta.co.uk

#Associations

Container leasing

Since the first use of containers for moving cargo in the 1950s, the container industry has grown to over 36 million TEUs today. A TEU is a twenty-foot equivalent unit, so a smaller container of 20 foot is one TEU, a large container of 40 foot is two TEUs. 18 million TEUs are leased together with 550,000 of the chassis units that hold them. The replacement value of the leased fleet is estimated at US$49 billion. A host of domestic and international laws, regulations, conventions and standards apply to this most international of industries.

The International Institute of Container Lessors is based in Washington DC and represents a dozen of the largest global lessors.
www.iicl.org

#Market

Contingent rentals

Lease payments that vary depending on factors defined in the lease agreement, such as the level of use of the asset.

#Accounting #Contract

Continuation

For lease accounting, a lease is assumed to be non-cancellable if the cost to the lessee to cancel is such that continuation of the lease is reasonably certain. More generally, the term can also refer to a lease entering a secondary period.

#Accounting #Contract

Contract hire

A lease agreement, typically for cars, which is bundled with services. For company car fleets the services might include maintenance, insurance, replacement vehicles and fleet administration. As it is a hire agreement, the assets are returned to the lessor at the end of the agreed period. For car fleets there will typically still be a substantial residual value, making the accuracy of forecasting used car prices critical to contract hire pricing and profitability.

#Products

Conversion rate

Proportion of quotations that are accepted and result in a lease contract being made.

#Operations

Corporate interest restriction rules

Tax rules, introduced in 2017 in the UK and across Europe, that restrict the interest cost that multinational companies may deduct from taxable profits. The rules are complex, but broadly limit interest expense to 30% of earnings before tax. This could affect the tax deductibility of interest on finance leases, but the threshold is so high that UK lessees are unlikely to be affected. There are concerns that some airline and shipping company lessees in Northern Europe (where finance leases are more commonly used for aircraft and ships) could be affected.

#Tax

Corporation tax

C

Taxes paid by companies on their taxable profits. Taxable profits are based on accounting profit with various adjustments. Depreciation is not allowable as an expense for tax purposes but instead tax capital allowances may be claimed.

#Tax

Cost / income

Operating expenses as a percentage of operating income. In the Leaseurope Index, the weighted average of all participating companies' cost/income ratios in 2017 was 48%. For the Leaseurope Index operating expenses excludes interest, and operating income includes net interest.

#Operations

Cost of capital

The cost of a firm's finance, calculated as a weighted average of debt and equity. The higher a firm's cost of capital, the more likely it is that leasing assets will be an attractive option. This is one reason lease Penetration rates for large listed companies are low on average but also vary considerably between firms.

#Finance

Cost of risk

Loan loss provisions as a percentage of average portfolio. In the Leaseurope Index, the average cost of risk for participating companies in 2017 was 0.3% This was lower than previous years, for example the average in 2015 was 0.5%.

#Operations #Risk

Co-terminous agreement

Where two or more leases are started at different times but have the same finish date. This may happen if, for example, a lessee wishes to add some extra cars to its fleet. It is more commonly found in the property rather than equipment leasing market.

#Contracts

County Court Judgement (CCJ)

A court ruling in favour of a legal entity claiming that monies owed to them have not been paid. It applies to both individuals and companies. Once the court order has been registered and is in the public domain, credit reference agencies will use this information to reassess that entity's credit-worthiness. In this way CCJs have a negative impact on an entity's credit score.

#Risk

Covenants

A clause in a contract that contains a restriction or a requirement or a commitment that certain acts will be performed. Bank loans may include covenants requiring borrowers to maintain minimum ratios of assets to liabilities or that restrict the firm's absolute level of liabilities.

In a lease agreement, the term can also refer more generally to the lessee's obligations e.g. to make rental payments and to maintain the assets.

#Contracts

Credit

Any kind of loan or other 'financial accommodation' that provides a right to defer repayment for goods or services or for lending of money. This includes any leasing agreement where the lessee has an option to buy the asset from the lessor. The purchase option can be set out in the lease agreement or separately. If there is no such option in a lease, the agreement will generally be one of hire and not credit.

#Conduct #Legal

Credit institution

C

Under European law, an authorised financial institution. A Capital Requirements Directive (CRD) credit institution is one that accepts deposits or other funds from the public and grants credits and is subject to prudential regulation.

Bank-owned lessors in the UK that are separate businesses to the bank and are not prudentially regulated are not classified as credit institutions for regulatory purposes. A different approach is taken by regulators in some other European countries, where such lessors would be classified as credit institutions, just not CRD credit institutions.

#Prudential

Credit loss

For accounting, the difference between the contracted and expected cashflows, including the lease rentals and any other income that is part of the credit provided. For IFRS 9, a loss allowance is made for this amount in the accounts. 12-month Expected Credit Losses ("12m ECL") is the proportion of lifetime expected credit losses that will probably be realised within the next 12 months.

#Accounting

Credit rating

An independent assessment of a company's creditworthiness. For the largest companies it is based on an expert assessment. For smaller companies it is typically an automated assessment based on available electronic data. It may be referred to as a 'credit score' or 'credit report' rather than credit rating. As most small companies now file only abbreviated accounts at Companies House the credit reference agencies tend to rely on non-accounting data when preparing credit reports.

#Credit

Credit risk

The possibility that a lessee could default on lease rental payments, leaving the lessor having to consider recovering and selling the asset or taking legal action to recover the amount owed.

#Credit #Risk

Credit sale

The sale of an asset with extended credit provided by the supplier. An alternative to leasing but found mainly in the consumer goods markets.

#Alternatives

Cross-border leasing

Contract where the lessee and lessor are in different countries, includes export leasing. Often, but not necessarily, the leased assets will be located in the lessee's home country.

#Market

Crowdfunding

A form of Alternative finance, where a project is financed through many small investments from many people, typically through an online portal.

It has been suggested that crowdfunding could disrupt the leasing market, reducing the importance of banks and even making it possible to offer leasing arrangements that might be considered too risky today, but there have been no signs of this happening so far.

#Alternatives

Crown Commercial Service (CCS)

An executive agency of the Government, sponsored by the Cabinet Office, that advises the public sector on procurement and carries out central purchasing on behalf of multiple departments. It is the latest in a line of efforts to improve the efficiency of public procurement, following the Government Procurement Service (GPS) and Buying Solutions.

The CCS's framework RM3781 provides customers across the whole of the public sector with access to multifunctional devices (MFDs) such as printers and photocopiers, managed print and records information management services, including related finance options. Contract RM3710 covers vehicle leasing and associated services including fleet management. Central Government departments are under increasing pressure to use the CCS-negotiated contracts to exploit the full potential buying power of the public sector.

#Public sector

Data protection

The regulations over how firms protect the privacy of individuals set out in the Data Protection Act 2018, which incorporate the requirements of the European Union's General Data Protection Regulations. Lessors need to register annually as data controllers with the Information Commissioner's Office as they are may be obtaining, recording, storing, updating and sharing personal information on individuals from lessees' businesses. See General Data Protection Regulation.

#Regulation

Dealer

Firms, other than manufacturers, that sell vehicles or equipment to businesses or individuals. They may offer finance options to their customers, either by introducing them to a finance company or through a broker. The term is typically used in the office equipment sector. See also Resellers.

#Intermediaries

Debt adjusting

For consumer credit regulation, the activity of negotiating with a lender or owner, on behalf of a borrower or hirer, the settlement of a regulated credit or hire agreement. Firms carrying out debt adjusting in the consumer credit market require specific FCA permission. Obtaining a settlement figure for an existing asset finance agreement on behalf of a regulated customer is generally considered to be debt adjusting, but not advising customers on how to obtain a settlement figure themselves.

D

#Conduct

Debt counselling

For consumer credit regulation, the activity of giving advice to a borrower about the settlement of a debt due under a credit agreement or giving advice to a hirer about the settlement of a debt due under a consumer hire agreement. Firms carrying out debt counselling in the consumer credit market require specific FCA permission. Setting out options available to the customer in a neutral way such that no advice or opinion is provided is not debt counselling.

#Conduct

Default

Failure to meet the terms of an agreement, for example not making lease payments. Under prudential accounting rules, the classification of agreements as being in default needs to consider the number of days past due (as a starting point, 90 days is often used) as well as the likeliness of the customer to pay.

#Credit

Default interest

Where a higher rate of interest is charged to a borrower who is in arrears. This is not common practice in leasing although a late payment fee may be charged by some lessors.

#Credit #Contracts

Deferred taxation

A deferred tax liability is an accounting provision for tax that is not due to be paid within the current year but may have to be paid at some future time. A deferred tax asset is a possible right to pay less tax in the future. For some lessors, including those with long-life assets such as railway rolling stock, significant deferred tax assets have arisen in the past through capital allowances carried forward from the year in which leased equipment was acquired.

#Accounting #Tax

Delinquent receivable

Payments that are overdue but not yet classed as defaulted. More commonly referred to as arrears. The expectation may still be that the amounts due will eventually be paid off.

#Credit

Department for Business, Energy and Industrial Strategy (BEIS)

Government department with responsibilities for business, industrial strategy, science, innovation, energy, and climate change. Renamed from the Department for Business, Innovation and Skills in 2016, when it was amalgamated with the Department for Energy and Climate Change.

Its Shareholder Executive agency manages the Government's support to businesses provided through the British Business Bank and its subsidiary the Startup Loans Company. Responsible for UK law on company reporting and audits, which for now follows EU directives.

#Bodies

Deposit

A payment made at the outset of a lease agreement which reduces the amount funded. The ongoing lease payments should be lower than if there was no deposit. Sometimes called an 'initial payment'. It serves to mitigate the lessor's risk caused by many assets being worth substantially less as soon as they are no longer new. See also Security deposit.

#Contracts

Depreciation

The reduction in an asset's value over time. Depreciation is charged as an operating expense in the lessee's income statement for assets under a finance lease, or the lessor's income statement for an operating lease. The two main methods of calculating depreciation are straight-line and reducing balance. The aim of either method is to realistically reflect the asset's current value to the business.

#Accounting

Difference in Charges commission

A method for calculating the commission paid to a broker by a lender. There are two variants.

Under an 'increasing Difference in Charges' model the lender sets a minimum charge rate for the proposed lease. The broker adds a margin to this to reach the charge rate to be quoted to the customer. In general, the difference between the two charge rates is the broker's commission.

A 'reducing Difference in Charges' commission is where the lender sets a maximum interest rate and the broker can choose whether to quote that to the customer or to reduce the rate (and earn less commission) to be more competitive.

The 'increasing' approach can be seen as controversial and has attracted some attention from the FCA for regulated consumer car finance agreements, as it creates a theoretical incentive for the broker to mislead a customer about the rates available in the market.

This potential conflict has largely been addressed by lenders either shifting to the 'reducing' model or imposing caps on the 'increasing' charge rate to customers. The competitive market also imposes a natural limit on rates that can be charged to lessees.

#Intermediaries

DIMS

Durable, Identifiable, Moveable and Saleable: The four traditional tests for whether an asset is suitable for leasing. It might be most accurate to identify them now as the tests of whether there is a hard asset.

#Assets

D   Direct debit

Using a mandate provided by the lessee, the arrangement by which lessors will usually collect lease payments from the lessee's bank account.

#Credit

Direct tax

Another name for corporation tax.

#Tax

Disadvantages of Leasing

As shown under the Advantages of leasing, the benefits of leasing vary between types of leases and the lessee's circumstances. The possible disadvantages to a potential lessee – which are often avoidable by selecting the most appropriate lessor and type of lease – might include:

- Higher cost than using retained earnings or bank loans to pay for assets due to any of the following:
- The firm having access to lower cost capital or loans than the interest rate inherent in the lease
- Additional fees and other charges for the lease e.g. administration, documentation, purchase option, renewal and insurance
- The firm having tax capacity, particularly for Annual Investment Allowances, but wishing to use a lease where capital allowances are not available to the lessee
- Having access to similar equipment at lower cost from other suppliers not offering leasing options.
- Non-pricing lease terms that might not suit the potential lessee's needs if not carefully selected:
- The risk that the firm will have to return equipment it still needs at the end of the lease if there is no purchase

option, or if the terms of the option are unattractive, or if the contract is not fully understood

D

- An end-date of the lease, or absence of a specific end-date, that could lead to a firm having to pay for equipment it might no longer need
- Conditions for returning equipment at end of lease that might be difficult to meet.
- Risks arising from associated parties:
- Accepting offers of additional benefits from intermediaries in Side-letters that might not be delivered
- Paying in advance for services or maintenance that might not be delivered by third-parties.

#Alternatives

Disclosed agency

See Agency agreement.

#Legal

Discount rate

The interest rate used to calculate a discounted cash flow. The rate is applied to future cash flows to state them in current prices. The discount rate seeks to remove the time value of money from future cash flows.

#Finance

Discounted cash flow

The present value of a series of future cash flow e.g. lease payments, calculated by applying a discount rate to the payments. It can be used in a lease vs. buy analysis for example. If a firm has surplus cash, a relevant rate might reflect the alternative ways in which that money could be used. Otherwise the relevant rate could be the cost of borrowing funds to buy, rather than lease, the asset.

#Finance

Distributor

Firm that distributes a manufacturer's goods to suppliers for onward sale to businesses or individuals. The distributor may work with a lessor to establish a vendor finance programme for use by dealers.

#Intermediaries

Double-dip lease

An international lease where, due to different tax rules in different countries, both the lessee and the lessor can claim capital allowances (or equivalent tax benefits) on the same equipment. Many tax authorities have taken steps to stop this happening.

#Tax

Drawdown

After a lease agreement has been agreed, the period over which the lessee completes the investment in leased equipment.

#Contracts

Dun & Bradstreet (D&B) Critical Intelligence System

Credit reference agency D&B runs a system allowing lessors to share suspicions on suspicious businesses in a secure and safe environment. Established with support from the FLA and following review of relevant legal aspects, the system is intended to allow the industry to share suspicions on suspected fraudsters and stops them from approaching different lessors until one offers finance. Information filed by participating lessors is also investigated by D&B specialists. The system helps lessors identify when to carry out additional anti-fraud checks. It can also help them to confirm that a business which might initially appear suspicious is genuine.

#Risk

Dual financing

See Multi-financing

#Risk

e-signatures

E

A digital equivalent to a 'wet ink' signature on a contract. These are now becoming commonly used in leasing, especially in the smaller ticket space. Whilst there has been some debate whether e-signatures are capable of meeting the statutory requirements, this is generally accepted by most funders for execution of simple contracts. However, some question marks remain with regards to documents which are executed as deeds e.g. personal guarantees. Also, if a contract involves a party outside of the UK, it is important to understand whether electronic execution is permissible in the relevant country.

The Law Commission is carrying out a consultation on electronic execution and responses to their initial consultation paper were submitted in November 2018.

#Contracts

Early settlement

Where a lease agreement is cancelled by the lessee before the end of the contracted primary or minimum period.

For a non-regulated credit agreement, the lessor is under no obligation to forego any of the lease payments due. In some circumstances lessors may voluntarily discount the total amount payable to exclude interest charges due for the remaining period of the lease.

For a regulated credit agreement (as defined by the Consumer Credit Act 1974) the lessee may terminate at any time (an 'Early termination'). If the payments made exceed half of the total amount payable, and the asset is in good condition, no further amounts are due. Otherwise the lessee will need to pay the sum needed to bring the total payments to that level.

#Contracts

Earnings before Interest and Tax (EBIT)

One way of measuring and reporting profit. It is often seen as the most useful measure of the underlying performance of a company, as it is not dependent upon changes in interest or tax rates that are outside of the company's control. Under IFRS 16, operating leases rentals for lessees will be split between interest and depreciation, which will have the effect of increasing EBIT compared to equivalent reporting under IAS 17.

#Accounting

Economic life

See Useful life.

#Assets

Economic owner

The party that enjoys the benefits of using an asset in its business and accepts the associated risks. Lease accounting and taxation rules are based on this concept as opposed to legal ownership. It is why the lessor as legal owner of an asset might not report the asset on its own balance sheet and might not be entitled to claim the tax capital allowances.

#Accounting #Tax

Educational and Skills Funding Agency (ESFA)

The executive agency of the Department for Education that manages finance for all state schools in England, allocating finance through local authorities as well as direct to academy schools.

The ESFA is particularly relevant for leasing by academy schools. Over half of all secondary schools are academies and the Government intends for most others to join them.

The ESFA issues an Academies Financial Handbook which states that academies may use operating leases but must seek ESFA approval before using finance leases. The ESFA has said that it will approve use of finance leases if they represent good value, but in practice few academies appear to have obtained such approval. In effect, therefore, academy schools are restricted to using operating leases, in line with local authority-funded schools. *https://www.gov.uk/government/organisations/education-and-skills-funding-agency#Public sector*

E

Embezzlement

Theft of a leased asset in situations where the contract was originally entered into lawfully, but a fraud occurs during the life of the contract. This often happens following a deterioration in the performance of the lessee's business. Embezzlement is a criminal offence.

#Risk

End-of-life functions

Activities to deal with the termination of lease contracts, including Settlements or Asset disposal.

#Operations

Endorsement

A variation or amendment to a lessor's standard lease agreement terms and conditions. The changes may be specified on a separate sheet or schedule, cross-referenced to the standard agreement and signed and dated by both parties at the same time as the main agreement. Simpler variations may be handled by deletions or amendments initialled by both parties.

#Contracts

Enhanced capital allowances

Where the Government allows businesses to claim capital allowances more quickly than normal. ECAs for eligible energy saving and water efficient technologies allow 100% capital allowances in the year of purchase. ECAs are also available for eligible investments in six regional enterprise zones. The

Annual Investment Allowance has the same effect. ECAs are useful for businesses with tax capacity using finance leases and hire purchase. They cannot be claimed by lessors other than for equipment they are using themselves.

#Tax

E

Equipment Leasing and Finance Association (ELFA)

The Washington DC-based trade association for the $1 trillion US equipment finance sector, including providers of leasing but also loans for buying assets and lines of credit used for equipment purchases. ELFA represents more than 600 member companies including national, regional and community banks, other financial services companies and manufacturers providing finance for equipment. In addition to its lobbying work it acts as the central resource for industry information, promotes the industry and is the forum for industry development including through its annual convention.
www.elfaonline.org

#Associations

Equipment Leasing and Finance Foundation

The US-based body that amongst other activities develops and publishes research relevant to the equipment finance industry. Established in 1989 by the Equipment Leasing and Finance Association, its trustees are appointed by the Association. It publishes the Journal of Equipment Lease Financing, State of the Industry reports, a monthly confidence index survey. Its Industry Future Council, comprising a cross-section of selected industry executives, explores current issues, trends, and the outlook for the future of the equipment finance industry.
www.leasefoundation.org

#Associations

Equipment Leasing Association

Set up in 1971 to represent the leasing industry by members of the Finance Houses Association, with which it shared premises and staff. From a base of 13 founder companies it grew to a membership of more than 70 lessors. It merged with the Finance Houses Association in 1992 to form the Finance and Leasing Association. The merger reflected the fact that both the FHA and the ELA were representing the business leasing market, although it left the UK without a dedicated leasing association.

#Associations

Equipment schedule

A document that may supplement a lease agreement especially where multiple items of equipment are involved. It contains details of the specific assets that will be leased, including for example the type of equipment, serial numbers, location and purchase price. Holding this information on a separate document is done for convenience, allowing the key terms and conditions of the lease to be agreed before the full details of the assets are known.

#Contract

Equity in a lease

The difference between the value of the leased assets and the minimum lease payments owed by the lessee. The equity should be broadly equivalent to the assets' residual value.

#Accounting

Ethics

The principles that govern standards of behaviour, for example honesty, trustworthiness, fairness and responsible lending.

According to the Banking Standards Board, established in 2015 to promote high standards of behaviour and competence across UK banks and building societies, it is not sufficient to follow laws and regulations. Firms and the individuals within them need to respect and live up to more generic standards, and not view legal or regulatory constraints as formalities or something to be gamed.

#Business

European Central Bank (ECB)

E

The central bank of the 19 European Union countries in the Eurozone. Its main task is to maintain price stability and so preserve the purchasing power of the single currency. Under the Single Supervisory Mechanism, from 2014 the ECB has directly supervised the most significant banks in the Eurozone and it oversees the supervision by national regulators of other banks. It is, therefore, the key prudential supervisor for many European bank lessors. The Bank of England and the ECB cooperate to help ensure a consistent approach to bank supervision.
www.ecb.europa.eu

#Bodies #Prudential

European Data Warehouse (EDW)

The European repository for loan-level data for Asset-Backed Securities (ABS) transactions. In 2018, it held and made publicly available detailed information on the loans supporting around 1,200 ABS transactions, including 200 classified as automotive (mostly consumer car loans and leases) and 40 leasing deals. The 40 leasing deals included around 0.5 million individual lease contracts provided to around 0.4 million borrowers.

It holds information on type of loan, loan size and balance, length of loan and maturity date, interest rate and arrears or losses. The identity of the borrower is not included. The EDW is run by the market and endorsed by the Eurosystem. For issuers who file information with the EDW their ABS should be eligible as collateral eligible European Central Bank schemes. Outside of Italy, the EDW is the only repository of shared lease performance information in Europe.
www.eurodw.eu

#Bodies #Funding

European Financial Reporting Advisory Group (EFRAG)

Association representing a range of European bodies that aims to represent the European public interest during the International Accounting Standards Board's development of changes to international accounting standards. Having earlier been critical of many aspects of the IASB's proposals for a new lease accounting standard, EFRAG eventually advised the European Commission that IFRS 16 was in the European public good.
www.efrag.org

#Accounting

European Investment Bank (EIB)

The European Union's Bank. The EIB is owned by the EU member states and provides finance for projects that support EU policy objectives. It borrows on the international capital markets at low rates because of the support provided by the EU national governments.

The EIB supports projects that make a significant contribution to growth and employment in Europe. Its intermediated loans and guarantee schemes are used by many leasing companies in Europe but mainly outside of the UK.

The EIB Loans for SMEs programme provides low cost funds to intermediary financial institutions for lending to small and medium-sized businesses. Participating lessors match the funds provided by the EIB, but not necessarily at the same rate. The benefit of the EIB's low cost finance is passed on to the lessee through a lower overall rate for the lease. The rate varies from case to case depending on the credit profile of the lessee or any other party that guarantees the loan, such as a parent bank.

The EIB also provides intermediated loans for other goals including promoting employment amongst mid-cap companies and promoting environmental sustainability.

The programmes have had relatively little use in the UK, in part reflecting the dominance of bank lending in the UK and banks' access to the Bank of England's credit easing schemes. Access to EIB funding may continue after the UK's planned exit from the EU as around 10% of the Bank's lending is outside of the EU.

www.eib.org

#Bodies

E   European Investment Fund (EIF)

Part of the European Investment Bank group, a specialist provider of risk finance to benefit small and medium-sized enterprises (SME) across Europe. Its shareholders are the European Investment Bank (EIB), the European Union, represented by the European Commission, and a wide range of public and private banks and financial institutions.

The EIF provides guarantees and credit enhancement to promote SME lending. Through its Structured Finance programme, it can facilitate the placement of debt with third party investors by guaranteeing the timely payment of debt's interest and principal. It can also share the risk on new leasing, in exchange for a fee, under its COSME Loan Guarantee Facility (formerly the Risk Sharing Instrument).

With EU support, the EIF provides uncapped guarantees to leasing companies on 50% of each eligible lease, potentially enabling lessors to offer finance for riskier asset classes or clients. Around €350 million of guarantees for leasing companies in Europe were approved between 2013 and 2015. As the role of independent leasing companies grows in Europe, it seems likely that the need for the EIF's guarantee support programmes will increase. Access to EIF support is not expected to continue after the UK's planned exit from the EU, however.

The EIF is supporting the British Business Bank's ENABLE Funding programme for lessors.

www.eif.org

#Bodies

Evergreen lease

A lease agreement that extends automatically for fixed periods until notice is given by the lessee to cancel it. Although there are circumstances where it may be a valid technique, there is a risk that the agreement will not suit the needs of lessees if they are not fully aware of how the arrangement works.

#Contracts

Export leasing

When a manufacturer offers leasing options to customers in other countries. It could offer leases itself as a captive lessor working on a cross-border basis, set up captive lessor operations in the destination countries, partner with lessors in the destination countries, or partner with one or more lessors that works on an international basis.

#Market

Extension rental

Where a lease continues beyond the initial Term, the value at which the rentals will be charged. It may simply be the same as the rentals during the initial term, or the contract might stipulate a specific Renewal option, which might be a lower or even a Peppercorn rent.

#Contracts

Facility letter

A document that sets out a commitment for the lessor to finance equipment subject to conditions such as security, timescale and payment of any fees. Most likely to be relevant to big-ticket leases.

#Legal

Factoring

A form of asset-based finance, loans that are secured against specific trade receivables. Factoring firms ('factors') often provide 70% to 85% of the value of invoices up-front. They take on debt management and collecting responsibilities. When the invoices are paid, the factoring company makes the remaining balance available to their client less their fees.

#Alternatives

Fair value

When underwriting a lease agreement, the lessor will want to know that the equipment price agreed between the potential lessee and the equipment supplier reflects the fair value, which is the price that a well-informed buyer would pay in a competitive market.

F

For lease accounting, the amount for which an asset could be sold in an arm's length transaction, with neither buyer nor seller under any compulsion to buy or to sell.

A fair value purchase option is where, in a hire purchase arrangement, the lessee has the option to acquire the asset at its market value at the time that the option is exercised.

A fair renewal value is an extension rental that is calculated based on the then current fair market value.

#Accounting #Contracts

Fees

Any extra amounts charged by the lessor over and above the lease rentals. Firms may variously charge documentation, annual, insurance, renewal or other fees.

For regulated credit, any such fees should be included in the Annualised Percentage Rate and explained to the lessee before the lease is agreed. A firm must not impose charges on customers in default or arrears difficulties unless the charges are no higher than necessary to cover the reasonable costs of the firm.

#Contracts #Conduct

Finance and Leasing Association (FLA)

Founded in 1992 with the merger of the Finance Houses Association and the Equipment Leasing Association. It is split into three divisions, representing consumer finance, motor finance and asset finance. The Association is principally a representative body for the consumer finance and leasing industries. It operates codes of conduct for its consumer and business lenders, reviews complaints received about its members, and organises training,

seminars and drinks receptions. Its Annual Dinner, held in February at the Grosvenor House Hotel, is one of the largest industry events of the year.
www.fla.org.uk

#Associations

Finance house

F

Traditionally, a non-bank finance company which funded consumer hire purchase agreements. More recently, any finance company specialising in hire purchase for both consumer and small business customers. The term is sometimes used interchangeably with 'lessor'.

#Market

Finance Houses Association

The former trade association for the instalment credit industry, its members provided hire purchase agreements mainly to consumers and smaller businesses. Founded in 1945, it merged with the Equipment Leasing Association in 1992 to form the Finance and Leasing Association. It established and ran the Finance Houses Diploma.

#Associations

Finance House Base Rate

An index maintained by the Finance and Leasing Association (FLA), the rate is calculated at the end of each month by averaging the cost of three-month money in the interbank market over the previous eight weeks. The resulting figure is then rounded up to the next half point. The FLA states that the process is entirely arithmetical and contains no discretionary element.

The index is used by some finance companies as a basis of calculating lending charges for mainly consumer agreements that are based on variable interest rates. It is not in common use in the business asset finance market. Most leasing agreements in the UK are fixed rate and where they are variable they tend to be based on the Bank of England base rate.

#Market

Finance Houses Diploma

F

The Finance Houses Association's, and later the Finance and Leasing Association's, courses and qualifications. Many of today's leaders of the industry hold the qualification. It was discontinued around 2001 due to falling registrations.

#Operations

Finance lease

For lease accounting under IAS 17, a lease that transfers substantially all of the 'risks and rewards' of ownership of an asset from the lessor to the lessee. This applies, for example, if ownership of the asset will transfer at the end of the lease, if there is a bargain purchase option, or if the lease can be extended at a rate below the market level. Other factors used to identify a finance lease include the length of the lease term compared to the economic life of the asset and the value of the minimum lease payments compared to the value of the asset.

Under IAS 17 finance leases are reported on the balance sheet of the lessee. This will continue under IFRS 16 although today's operating leases will also be reported in a similar way, removing the distinction between the two types for lessee accounting for IFRS users.

Also known as a capital lease, especially in the US.

#Accounting #Products

Financial Accounting Standards Board (FASB)

The body that establishes financial accounting and reporting standards for use by US companies. The FASB has developed a new lease accounting standard in a joint project with the IASB.

The two bodies will, however, operate their own separate lease accounting standards.
www.fasb.org

#Accounting #Bodies

Financial Conduct Authority (FCA)

One of the regulators of the UK's financial services industry, working alongside the Prudential Regulatory Authority (PRA) and the Bank of England.

Financial services firms must be authorised by the FCA. They are listed on the FCA's Register, must follow the relevant parts of the FCA's Handbook of rules covering how they conduct their business, and report on their activities using the FCA's Gabriel system.

The most direct impact for lessors is on their conduct of business of regulated consumer credit agreements, but the FCA's Principles for Business apply across all activities of authorised firms. The Principles include the need to conduct business with integrity, due skill, care and diligence.
www.fca.org.uk

#Bodies #Conduct

Financial Intermediary & Broker Association (FIBA)

A new trade association representing commercial finance brokers (who may deal in asset finance) alongside bridging loan professionals, residential mortgage brokers, and independent financial advisers.

#Associations

Financial Ombudsman Service (FOS)

Independent body with statutory powers to help settle individual disputes between consumers or small businesses and finance companies. It is paid for by the Financial Services industry through a levy on FCA-regulated firms.

Since 2014 'micro-enterprises' with fewer than ten employees can bring complaints about FCA-regulated firms to the FOS.

95% of UK businesses qualify. The complaint must first have been considered through the firm's own complaints procedure. Regulated firms pay a flat rate of £550 for each complaint investigated by the FOS, in addition to the levy. Lessors dealing with regulated customers must inform customers they will have the option of using the FOS.

F

The FOS does not publish the outcome of individual investigations. Its quarterly newsletter includes a range of case studies. Its annual report includes statistics on number of complaints handled by product. In the year to March 2018 there were 5,800 complaints about hire purchase products, up 72% on the previous year, and 1,600 complaints about hiring, leasing and renting, up 15%. Most of these complaints are likely to have been from consumers rather than small businesses.
www.financial-ombudsman.org.uk

#Bodies #Conduct

Financial Reporting Advisory Board (FRAB)

Independent body established by HM Treasury to advise Government on financial reporting. In recent years the FRAB has considered how local authority schools should distinguish between operating and finance leases. The FRAB will influence how IFRS 16 is applied in the UK public sector.

#Accounting #Public sector

Financial Reporting Council (FRC)

Body that develops and enforces financial reporting standards in the UK, it incorporates the former Accounting Standards Board.
www.frc.org.uk

#Accounting

Financial Reporting Standards

The UK accounting rules followed by all companies other than those using international financial reporting standards. The key standard is FRS 102 which consolidated more than 70 topic-specific standards including the former leases standard SSAP 21.

Small companies may be eligible to follow special rules for smaller firms that are included in a section of FRS 102, or the separate micro-entities standard FRS 105.

Before SSAP 21 was withdrawn, many accountants in the industry used accompanying guidance that had been issued by the Finance and Leasing Association in 2000. The Statement of Recommended Practice (SORP) 'Accounting issues in the asset finance and leasing industry' was endorsed by the Accounting Standards Board and its parent the Financial Reporting Council. The SORP was withdrawn by the FRC when FRS 102 took effect but still provides some useful insights into how to apply the lease accounting rules.

For now, the UK Standards have not been changed to reflect the new lease accounting approach of IFRS 16. The Financial Reporting Council consulted on making changes for consistency with IFRS 16 in 2017. It concluded that further analysis was needed before any firm proposals could be made. It seems likely that new proposals will now be considered in 2020 or 2021, based on the first two years' experience of large firms using IFRS 16.

#Accounting

Fintech

Refers to technological innovation in the financial services sector. The term may be associated with radical innovation which has the potential to disrupt existing business models in financial markets.

Fintech has had limited impact on the leasing market to date, but it has the potential to deliver major changes, either directly to the leasing business model or indirectly by making other forms of business finance more attractive.

Solutions that have been tested or proposed include: 'automated brokers' by matching needs of small businesses with funders; peer-to-peer lending platforms for leasing; marketplace lending platforms that match institutional investors with funders; and various 'onboarding' platforms that claim to use unconventional metrics to underwrite loans or combine a range of metrics from different sources into one seamless check.

#Business

F

Fittings

Items in buildings that are free standing or hung by screws, nails or hooks. For tax purposes, they may be categorised as either Plant and machinery and eligible for capital allowances, or Fixtures and not then eligible for capital allowances. HMRC provides detailed guidance on the correct categorisation.

#Tax

Fixed assets

Items of plant, property and equipment used by a business for more than one accounting period and recognised on the user's balance sheet. They may be used for the purposes of production, the supply of goods or services, rental to others, or administration.

#Accounting

Fixed charge

A form of security which gives the charge holder the right to have a particular asset or assets and their sales proceeds appropriated to discharge a debt. It is not ownership of an asset but an 'encumbrance' on the asset. Because a lessor already owns an asset being leased, they cannot charge the asset. However, the lessor might require a fixed charge against another asset as extra security, perhaps where the asset being leased has limited resale value. A fixed charge has the advantage of ranking before a floating charge in the order of repayment on an insolvency.

#Legal

Fixed rate

A lease where the lease payments do not fluctuate with changes in interest rates. Most lease agreements with smaller businesses are on fixed rates (although there may be a clause allowing upward adjustments if UK tax rates increase).

#Contracts

Fixed term rental

A lease where the equipment is expected to be returned to the lessor at the end of the lease period, there being no other contractual option. This does not prevent the lessor then negotiating further rentals or selling the ex-lease equipment to the former lessee at a realistic market value. Fixed term rental tends to be used in support of vendor programmes, as the vendors' aim would be to replace old equipment for new.

#Products

Fixtures

Assets that become an integral part of the buildings in which they are installed.

If classified as fixtures, leased assets may be difficult to remove and, therefore, provide little or no security. A landlord's waiver might be required to facilitate removal.

For accounting, an agreement for leasing an asset that is a fixture would almost certainly be classified as a finance rather than operating lease.

For tax purposes, a fixture would normally not be classified as Plant and Machinery, and so would not be eligible for capital allowances. HMRC provides guidance on 'integral fixtures' that would qualify for capital allowances, including for example escalators and external solar heating.

#Accounting #Assets #Tax

Flat rate

The interest charge for a lease calculated by dividing the interest charged per year by the amount financed (typically the cost of the asset less any deposit). The converse, which is less commonly used, is a reducing balance rate, where the interest charged is divided by the net book value of the lease in each year.

#Finance

Fleet

The company car and van fleet market is one of the largest segments of the UK leasing industry. More than half of all new cars sold in the UK are purchased for the fleet market. The largest fleet lessors, according to the Asset Finance 50, are Leaseplan, Lex, Alphabet, ALD and Arval.

#Market

Floating charge

A charge over all the assets of a company, or a class of those assets, rather than a Fixed charge over a specific asset or assets. A floating charge ranks after a Fixed charge in the order of repayment on an insolvency.

#Legal

Foreign Account e Tax Compliance Act (FATCA)

The United States' Foreign Account Tax Compliance Act (FATCA), requires that foreign financial Institutions and certain other bodies report to the US Government on the foreign assets held by their US account holders. It means that if a US business has leased assets in the UK, details might need to be reported unless various exemptions and exclusions apply. Captive finance companies are excluded. Reporting is bi-annual, online via HM Revenue and Customs.

#Tax

Fraud

Intentional misrepresentation, concealment or other deceit to the detriment of another person.

Lessors are at risk from many types of fraud. Risk officers might say there is nothing new under the sun in asset finance fraud. The risk of fraud can be mitigated greatly but there is always a trade-off between attempting to completely remove risk and keeping down the costs of providing a good customer service.

Most fraud originates from customers or from intermediaries and suppliers.

Customer fraud is often in the form of false information in finance applications. The risk can be mitigated through identity and address verification, obtaining credit references, CIFAS and Dun & Bradstreet Critical Intelligence System checks, asset inspections, asset valuation checks, and procedures to sense-check equipment requirements against the profile of the applicant's business.

F

Fraud by broker or vendor intermediaries can be difficult to identify, particularly if the customer is complicit. Mitigants include appraisal of new intermediaries, on-site reviews of existing intermediaries, controls on payouts including checking bank accounts, and only paying direct to the appropriate parties once the equipment is confirmed as satisfactorily delivered.

Like any business, a lessor is also subject to the risk of internal fraud by its own staff or contractors. Mitigants include requiring multiple sign-offs for large transactions and segregation of duties.

In recent years some of the largest frauds suffered by the industry have been caused by multi financing fraud (where the same asset is funded by more than one lessor) or Side-letters.

#Risk

Full payout lease

A lease where the agreed lease payments in the initial lease term are sufficient to pay for the asset, interest, other costs and the margin for the lessor. When pricing a full-payout lease the lessor does not rely on the asset having residual value or on there being a secondary period.

#Products

Full service lease

Lease where the lessor provides maintenance, repair and insurance. More frequently referred to as Contract hire.

#Products

Funder

Another name for a lessor. If there is one or more intermediate lessor/s, the underlying Funder is the Head lessor.

#Market

Funding

F

How a lessor raises cash for leasing assets. The options include use of deposits for a bank, using own equity, or borrowing the funds to lend. Borrowing options include Block discounting, issuing Commercial paper, Securitisation, use of the Bank of England's Funding for Lending Scheme or Term Funding Scheme, or use of relevant British Business Bank and European Investment Bank schemes.

#Funding

Funding for Lending Scheme (FLS)

Scheme launched by the Bank of England and HM Treasury in 2012. It is intended to encourage banks to lend more to UK households and businesses.

Participating banks borrow UK Treasury Bills in exchange for eligible collateral. The banks can then use the Bills as collateral for borrowing cash, either in the money markets or from the Bank of England. Banks also have the option of holding the Bills to meet their liquidity requirements under prudential requirements, which frees up their cash reserves for lending. The amount and rate paid for the Bills depends on the quantity of lending relative to earlier periods.

The exclusion of non-banks from FLS led to concerns that FLS was distorting competition, not least in the leasing market. A partial response from the BoE was to allow participating banks to lend to non-bank finance companies. Use of this facility in the leasing industry appears to have been rare.

The FLS Extension announced in 2013 made use of the Scheme less attractive in the consumer markets. This placed greater emphasis on SME lending, possibly to the further detriment of lessors not eligible to participate. The Scheme closed for new drawings from January 2018, replaced by the Term Funding Scheme.

#Funding

General Data Protection Regulation (GDPR)

The new European data protection laws that took effect in May 2018. In the UK, they were enacted through the Data Protection Act 2018. For lessors and intermediaries, the new rules (aimed at providing more protection for individuals) are generally consistent with the tone of those in the pre-existing UK data protection legislation, but (like so much regulation facing lessors) now with tighter compliance rules, including enhanced obligations concerning record keeping. GDPR impacts business leasing in so far as firms hold data that identifies living individuals. It requires firms to issue privacy notices to customers, protect the data they hold from loss or misuse, and in relevant circumstances, to enable individuals to access their data and to have it corrected or erased.

When GDPR was implemented, there was some confusion about whether firms need to obtain express consent from individuals to hold their data. Providing the data relates to the provision of services (e.g. broking or lending) most firms now consider that this is not required.

The new rules have been quite problematic for introducers, as they must not only issue their own privacy information but often also that of the funders. The Information Commissioner's Office has agreed with the NACFB and FLA that intermediaries may provide website links to privacy policies of funders, rather than maintain stocks of each firm's paperwork.

#Regulation

Gross investment in the lease

For lease accounting, the sum of the lease payments that the lessee will pay the lessor under a finance lease, together with the expected residual value of the asset.

#Accounting

Guarantee

An undertaking to answer for the payment of a debt, or the performance of any other type of obligation, in the event of the default of another person primarily responsible for it.

#Credit

Hard assets

H

A term used by lessors to refer to assets that meet the DIMS (Durable, Identifiable, Moveable and Saleable) criteria. Assets are generally classified as either hard or soft, but there may be many different views on how to draw a line between the two types.

#Assets

Head lessor

The lessor that owns the asset and leases it to one or a series of intermediate lessors, which may then lease it on to a customer on either a disclosed or undisclosed agency basis.

#Legal #Market

Healthcare Financial Management Association

Professional body for finance staff working in UK hospital trusts and the wider healthcare industry. It provides technical briefings to many NHS finance directors including on leasing.
www.hfma.org.uk

#Public sector

Hell or high water

Standard term in lease agreement that confirms the unconditional obligation of the lessee to pay rents for any equipment element for the duration of the agreement, regardless of any event affecting wider aspects of the overall agreement, for example the failure of the maintenance provider.

#Legal

High net worth

For consumer credit regulation, an exemption that may apply where the customer earns more than £150,000 and/or has net assets excluding their main residence of more than £500,000. The term is also used more generally by lessors to refer to wealthy customers, including both individuals and small businesses.

#Conduct

High value leases

H

See Big-ticket.

#Market

Hire

For consumer credit law, a lease agreement where the lessee has no option to buy the asset from the lessor at the end of the lease. If there is any purchase option, whether it is written into the lease agreement or offered separately, it is a credit and not a hire agreement.

#Legal #Conduct

Hire purchase

An arrangement that gives the lessee an option to buy the asset from the lessor at the end of the lease period, provided the lessee has kept to the terms of the agreement. Hire purchase accounts for around 50% of the UK leasing market by value.

Although there is not an obligation to take up the option to purchase, there is often a Bargain purchase option so it is likely to be exercised.

For tax an agreement is only treated as hire purchase if there is a bargain purchase option. For consumer credit hire purchase is a form of credit and not hire, regardless of the cost of the purchase option.

#Products #Tax

HM Revenue and Customs (HMRC)

The UK tax authority, responsible for the administration and collection of tax including corporation tax. Its internal manual, Business Leasing, is published on the www.gov.uk website. The manual is intended to provide HMRC personnel with an introduction to lease accounting and lease accounting taxation, with special emphasis on the leasing of plant or machinery. The size of the manual leaves no doubt about the complexity of the UK's lease taxation rules.

#Tax

HM Treasury (HMT)

Government department that sets economic and financial policy, including the tax, financial conduct and prudential rules which are implemented by HM Revenue and Customs, the Financial Conduct Authority and the Prudential Regulation Authority. Oversees public spending, including capital spending across Government departments and initiatives including the Funding for Lending Scheme and the British Business Bank's schemes.

#Bodies

Holdback

Where the lessor retains part of the cost price of equipment until the end of the lease contract, rather than paying it all at the outset. This method can be used to support an arrangement where the lessor agrees to loosen its usual criteria for lessee eligibility, to support the supplier's sales. The amounts retained form a loss pool to cover the extra risk if this is realised. Also referred to as retention.

#Contracts #Risk

Holiday

Where a lessor permits a lessee to miss a certain number of payments. The missed payments, with additional interest, may be added to the end of the lease. Alternatively, the remaining lease payments may be adjusted upwards.

#Contracts

HPI

Supplier of data solutions to the car market, including a register that lessors can use to show their ownership of leased assets. See Asset registration.

#Assets

Hurdle rate

The minimum required rate of return for an investment project in a discounted cash flow analysis. If the cost of a project is too high, possibly due to the interest rate inherent in the lease, then it may fall short of the hurdle rate. A lower rate should, therefore, result in more investment taking place, everything else being equal.

#Finance

IAS 17

The former international accounting standard for leases, replaced by IFRS 16 for reporting periods ending from January 2019. First published in 1982, it was effective from 1984 and was revised in 2003.

#Accounting

IFRS 9

The international accounting standard for financial instruments that took effect in January 2018. It sets the rules for how banks and other financial institutions should measure financial assets and liabilities.

The key relevance to leasing, as compared to the previous rules under IAS 39, is the tighter impairment rules that determine how contacts that might fall into default or loss should be reported. Under the new "expected loss" model, firms must now report based on the forecast risk of defaults, rather than (only) historical trends.

For most leasing firms the effect of the change on the accounts is limited, as the probability of future losses is likely to be aligned with historic levels. However, the evidence needed to support the forecasts is more substantial, requiring analysis of both internal and external (e.g. general economic) factors. This aligns accounting with prudential regulation, as firms using the Advanced Internal Ratings Based method will already have models based on a similar approach.

For non-banks or banks using the Standardised approach for prudential regulation, the extra data and analysis involved can be substantial. Some may take the view that it is most efficient to treat leasing as part of a wider portfolio of SME lending. However, for firms able to collect sufficient leasing-specific data, IFRS 9 may help to demonstrate the lower risk advantages of leasing compared to other forms of lending.

#Accounting

IFRS 15

The international accounting standard for revenue recognition that took effect in January 2018. Revenue should be recognised when a 'performance obligation' is satisfied by transferring a promised good or service to a customer.

It has limited impact on lessors, as IFRS 16 determines the revenue recognition for lease contracts. It may impact reporting of non-lease revenue, for example maintenance or other services connected to leases.

#Accounting

IFRS 16

The new international accounting standard for leases, published in January 2016. It is effective from January 2019. It is the outcome of the IASB's project to improve lease accounting started in 2006.

For the lessee, IFRS 16 removes the distinction between operating leases and finance leases. Instead there will be only a single type of lease, the 'right of use' lease, which will be reported as an asset on the lessee's balance sheet.

The IASB decided that changing lessor accounting was unnecessary. Lessors will still report operating lease assets on their own balance sheets using rules very like IAS 17.

The 'right of use' model is controversial. A business leasing equipment will report a new asset on its balance sheet, whereas another business buying a service that uses identical equipment will not. In addition, both the lessee and the lessor will report the asset on their balance sheets, raising further doubts over whether this is an improvement over IAS 17.

#Accounting

Implicit lease rate

For lease accounting, the interest rate that when applied to the agreed lease payments at the start of the agreement will discount those payments to the cost of the equipment leased less any expected residual value. May also be referred to as the 'rate implicit in the lease' or the 'effective interest rate'.

#Accounting

In-life functions

Activities involved in managing existing lease agreements, including any required asset, contract, customer or supplier management.

#Operations

Indemnity

An undertaking by one person to meet the identified potential liability of another. Lessors will generally include an indemnity clause in the lease agreement under which the lessee accepts responsibility for all risks associated with the asset during the lease agreement. The lessee agrees, for example, to pay any legal expenses or penalties, if someone is injured when using the asset. A company director or sister company may indemnify the lessor in relation to any amounts owed by the lessee; this often forms part of a guarantee.

#Legal

Independent lessor

The term is used in two main ways. First, a lessor that is not a captive, so is free to offer finance on any make of equipment. Second, and more commonly in the UK, a lessor that is neither a captive nor a bank-owned leasing company.

#Market

I

Information Commissioner's Office (ICO)

The UK's regulator of information rights, including Data Protection and freedom of information. Lessors need to register as data controllers with the ICO. Sharing of data on individuals with credit reference agencies and for fraud avoidance purposes should follow ICO guidelines. The ICO has played a major role in the recent introduction of the European General Data Protection Regulations into the UK through the Data Protection Act 2018. *www.ico.org.uk*

#Regulation

Initial direct costs

In lease accounting, the costs of obtaining a lease that would not otherwise be incurred. For the lessee, they might include delivery or installation. For the lessor, they might include broker commissions.

#Accounting

Insolvency

The inability of a company to meet its debts as they become due. An insolvent business can be placed into administration or wound up. Administration allows for the reorganisation of the company with a moratorium placed over existing debts. A winding up is done using either a creditors' voluntary liquidation or a compulsory liquidation. It leads to the dissolution of the company. See Administration order.

#Risk

Insolvency Practitioner (IP)

An individual who is licensed and authorised to act in relation to a party facing insolvency, be it an individual, partnership or company. They assess that party's current financial standing, the extent of their indebtedness to various creditors and their ability to repay the debt. They often have the authority to dispose of certain assets to mitigate the party's overall indebtedness.

In carrying out their duties, IPs must decide at what stage to contact any lessors with interests in a case. They may contact a lessor at an early stage if they are confident they can easily reach a designated individual who has experience in dealing with insolvencies and can be expected to cooperate with the IP's efforts to maintain the business as a going concern.

#Risk

Inspection

Lessors may choose to inspect larger assets in particular before agreeing to lease them. Various options are available in the market, including using own staff, asking a broker to inspect, or using a third-party inspection service. The inspection might cover the condition of the asset itself as well as the physical space in which it is located as this can provide indications of a fraud.

#Assets #Risk

Instalment credit

Form of credit where the borrower repays the loan over time in equal instalments. The loan may be for the purpose of buying an asset, in which case the borrower owns the asset from the outset.

#Alternatives

Institutional investors

Financial services firms that invest money on behalf of individuals or businesses. Includes pension funds, insurance companies, unit and investment trusts, and venture capitalists. In the US, institutional investors are a major source of funding for the leasing industry.

#Funding

Insurance

The lessee will usually be required to insure leased assets. The insurance should generally cover the replacement value of the asset against a range of defined risks, including fire, theft and damage. The lessor will usually be entitled to ask to see the policy. If the lessee does not show that a suitable policy is in place the contract may permit the lessor to add the cost of insurance to the lessee's payments (although for FCA regulated contracts, care would need to be taken to ensure this extra cost had been disclosed at the outset of the agreement).

#Contracts

Intangible assets

A non-physical asset, such as licences, brand names and trademarks. It is difficult for lessors to lease intangible assets as the nature of the asset means they can provide limited or no security.

#Assets

Interest

The price of money over time. Lessors pay interest for their borrowed funds and charge interest on their leases.

#Funding #Finance

Interest free

See Zero percent finance and Subsidy.

#Market

Interest rate risk

Risk that arises from changing interest rates. For a lessor, it is principally the risk that having lent at one rate, it will need to raise funds at a higher rate during the term of the agreement. To mitigate the risk, lessors can borrow for terms equivalent to their lending, or hedge against changes to rates. For a lessee, it is the risk that rates may increase, which is mitigated by agreeing a fixed rate contract.

#Funding #Risk

Internal financing

Where a firm purchases an asset using funds produced from its own operations, rather than external financing such as leasing.

#Alternatives

International Finance and Leasing Association (IFLA)

An association of leasing companies from around the world. It aims to be a platform for sharing industry information and best practices. It does not intend to be a representative body. There is a limit of one company per country and in 2018 there were 23 members, mostly from Europe with the UK member being Allied Irish Bank. The US is represented by the Equipment Leasing and Finance Association rather than by a company. The IFLA has its own song, sung to Andrew Lloyd Webber's "Amigos Para Siempre" ("Friends for Life").
www.ifla.com

#Associations

International leasing

An agreement where the asset is located in a different country to where the agreement is transacted. This leads to a wide range of extra considerations for lessors covering areas such as legal rights, tax, foreign exchange risk and social and political risk.

Most international leasing takes place out of countries with the lowest corporate tax rates, including Ireland.

#Market

Internet of Things (IoT)

The use of networking components, including sensors and transmitters, placed in assets to transmit data about that asset and how it is working. Sensors in many commercial and agricultural vehicles, for example, help optimise the efficiency both of the vehicle and of the job it is being used for.

The IoT makes leasing more complex as many assets now comprise a combination of the core equipment together with networking equipment and software applications. The equipment is also likely to have a longer useful life than the IoT technology. Some large lessors are developing innovative financing solutions for this problem, in conjunction with equipment manufacturers and distributors.

#Business

Introducer Appointed Representative (IAR)

For the FCA regulation of consumer credit, an Appointed Representative who is limited to effecting introductions, including providing customer's contact details to an authorised firm and distributing promotional material. An IAR should not discuss finance options with their customer.

#Intermediaries #Conduct

Invoice discounting

A type of factoring where the factor lends money to the firm but the firm continues to collect the money itself rather than having the factor do this.

#Alternatives

Invoice fraud

Where an inaccurate invoice is provided by a supplier or the supplier's invoice is altered in an attempt to defraud the lessor. There are many possible variations. The value of the asset and the deposit paid might be altered to make it appear the lessee has paid a larger deposit than in reality. The supplier might issue an invoice for new equipment when used equipment has been supplied.

#Risk

Joint Money Laundering Steering Group (JMLSG)

A working group made up of the UK's financial services trade associations, the JMLSG publishes guidance on how to interpret and apply the UK money laundering regulations. It includes a chapter dealing with leases which was updated in May 2018. The chapter identifies features of asset finance that can increase or decrease the risk of money-laundering or terrorist funding. These include:

- Paying lease rentals over a medium-term period provides a very slow means of 'layering' (using transactions to make it difficult to trace an illegal source of cash) the proceeds of crime (a feature suggesting low risk)
- The amount of asset finance obtainable is generally limited by the financial situation of the customer, limiting the possibility of layering a lot of money to financially stronger businesses (low risk)
- Customers must acquire business assets, which may be soft assets with low resale value (low risk), hard assets with reliable resale value (medium risk), or be luxury assets that might be desirable to criminals in their own right such as luxury cars (high risk)
- The lessor usually pays the supplier of the goods directly (low risk) but sometimes may pay the customer (medium risk)
- Rental payments are generally paid by direct debit from a UK bank account (low risk) but might be paid by cash (high risk)

- Any overpayments will generally be reimbursed to the business named on the agreement (low risk) but might be requested to be paid to a third party (high risk)

The guidance suggests that lessors should assess:
- The suitability of the asset for the customer
- The credentials of the Vendor of the asset.
- For sale and leaseback contracts, the original invoices and the credentials of the supplier of assets
- The reasons for an unusually early termination of a lease agreement, as this could be a sign of layering.

Overall the JMLSG notes that the features of asset finance make it a 'low risk' of money laundering or terrorist financing, providing sensible credit policies and procedures are followed based on the above features.

Firms regulated by the Financial Conduct Authority must follow the FCA's handbook, including its Financial Crime Guide. Firms may not rely only on the JMLSG guidance to ensure compliance with the FCA handbook or the underlying legal obligations. The FCA has confirmed it will consider the JMLSG guidance when deciding whether a firm has breached the regulations, although it is not legally obliged to do so.

www.jmlsg.org.uk

#Bodies #Regulation

Kickback

Fraudulent practice by which, for example, an equipment supplier might incentivise a broker to misrepresent a deal. For example, the broker could knowingly pass a false invoice to the finance company, and in return receive a cash payment from the supplier.

#Risk

Know Your Customer (KYC)

Due diligence checks that should take place when a customer first deals with a firm as part of firms' anti-money laundering procedures. The Joint Money Laundering Steering Group guidance sets out suggested checks.

#Regulation

Landlord's waiver

An agreement between the lessor and the landlord of the lessee's business premises. It allows the lessor to enter the premises to inspect and/or remove leased assets. It usually compels the landlord to refrain from creating security or other encumbrances (legal claims) involving the assets. Without a waiver the terms of the lessee's property lease might prevent the lessor accessing the assets if they could be classified as fixtures of the building.

Landlords can be resistant to signing waivers. If a lessor still wishes to proceed with a lease they can seek to protect themselves by issuing a formal notification of the existence of the lease to the landlord after the event, which prevents a landlord claiming to be unaware of the lessor's ownership of an asset.

#Legal

Lease

Agreement by which the owner of the asset (the 'lessor') allows another party (the 'lessee') to use an asset in return for payment. Some would use the term to refer specifically to hire agreements that have no purchase option, but a wider definition may also apply. See Leasing.

#Market

Lease payments

The amounts paid by the lessee to the lessor during the term of the lease agreement. May also be referred to as rentals, although lease payments may also include fees and other charges.

#Contracts

Lease purchase

A lease where title is expected to transfer to the lessee. Equivalent to a hire purchase with a bargain purchase option. For accounting, tax, VAT and legal purposes it is assumed that the purchase option will be taken and therefore the transaction is regarded as a sale.

#Products

Lease rate factor

The regular lease payment amount as a percent of the total cost of the leased equipment. It is a measure of limited use, since on its own it gives no reliable indication of the interest rate inherent in the lease.

#Contracts

L

Lease term

The minimum period for which the lessee agrees to lease an asset from the lessor. Also referred to as the non-cancellable period, primary lease period or minimum term. For lease accounting, the lease term will vary from the minimum period if the lessee has an option to extend or terminate a lease and is reasonably certain to exercise that option.

#Accounting #Contracts

Lease vs. buy

The technique of comparing leasing and purchasing options by considering the cashflows, including the tax effects, and discounting them to present value. Rather than carry this out for every asset, many larger businesses develop and review a leasing policy on a regular basis. They consider factors including the availability and cost of cash, tax, and the wider advantages and possible disadvantages of leasing.

#Finance

Lease with sales agency

Lease agreement where at the end of the lease term the lessee is automatically appointed as the lessor's agent to dispose of the ex-lease equipment. The agent is usually entitled to a rebate of rentals equivalent to the major element of the proceeds.

#Products

Lease with secondary rental

Lease agreement where at the end of the lease term the lessee can continue to rent the equipment at a nominal annual fee (the historic standard for small ticket leases is the equivalent of the previous monthly rental, but only annually). This preserves the hiring relationship and can continue for as long as the customer wishes to retain the equipment. The product tends to be used with higher value assets e.g. trucks. It is a form of Full Payout Lease.

#Products

Leaseurope

The umbrella trade body representing the leasing and automotive rental industries in Europe. Its members are the national trade associations across 33 countries in Europe. Founded in 1972 as the European Federation of Leasing Company Associations. UK member bodies are the FLA and BVRLA.

Based in Brussels, Leaseurope is governed by a Board of 12 heads of leasing firms that meets quarterly and by a General Assembly consisting of all member bodies that meets annually.

The Annual Convention, held each year over two days in October, is the largest gathering of senior leasing industry practitioners from across Europe.

www.leaseurope.org

#Associations

Leaseurope Index

Leaseurope's quarterly survey of European leasing and automotive rental companies. In addition to volumes and portfolios, the survey tracks cost/income, profitability, cost of risk, return on assets and return on equity ratios.

www.leaseurope.org

#Operations

Leasing

In law, a leasing contract is a relationship of 'bailment', meaning there is a temporary transfer of assets from one person to another. Similarly, for accounting purposes under international accounting rules, a leasing contract gives the 'right of use' of an asset to another person.

So is any contract of 'bailment' in law, or one that provides the 'right of use' for accounting purposes, leasing?

In common use of the term 'leasing' it is usual to exclude short-term rentals from the definition of the leasing market. There is no clear line but bailments of less than 12 months are generally considered to be part of the short-term rental market rather than leases. Under the new international lease accounting standard, IFRS 16, lessees will have the option not to report leases of less than 12 months on their balance sheets.

It is common to focus on business, rather than individual consumer, leasing when discussing the leasing market. It is also common to include the services that often accompany the bailment of an asset.

Leasing is not a term defined in law and regulations. There are in fact a host of different types of bailment arrangements in common use. Some include the word 'lease', others do not. Two specific types are: Hire Purchase and Conditional Sale. A traditional view, therefore, would be that leasing excludes these products. However, this does not fit with accounting standards and neither is it fully aligned with tax rules, so it can be useful to consider them as part of the wider leasing market.

It is also suggested that it can be useful to consider all bailment arrangements of similar characteristics as being part of the leasing market.

#Market

Leasing Broker Federation

Membership organisation supporting car and van leasing brokers and small fleet operating companies. The Federation was launched in 2015 and is run by Business Car Manager Ltd. It has around 100 members.
www.leasingbrokernews.co.uk

#Associations

Leasing Foundation

UK-based body set up to support the leasing and asset finance industry in the UK and internationally. It aims to carry out research, help the development of people in the industry and carry out charitable work. In addition to the directors, there is a board of around 40 Governors (senior influencers in the industry), a grouping of 130 Fellows (leading thinkers in the industry), Associates (industry professionals who wish to support the Foundation but do not yet wish to become Fellows) and Advisers (those who provide specialist expertise to the industry from outside). The Foundation's activities include an annual conference; an active networking and development group, Women in Leasing; a future leadership development programme; an MBA programme launched in 2016; research studies and lectures.
www.leasingfoundation.org

#Associations

Leasing Life

Trade publication owned by information solutions and technologies company Timetric. The monthly magazine is focused on the UK but includes coverage of the wider European market. It covers equipment leasing and another Timetric publication Motor Finance covers car leasing. Runs an annual European awards dinner.
www.leasinglife.com, www.motorfinanceonline.com

#Market

Leasing World

Independent trade publication founded in 2005. There is a monthly printed magazine with a digital edition. In 2012 launched Broker World, aimed at asset finance brokers. Runs an annual UK awards dinner.
www.leasingworld.co.uk, www.broker-world.com

#Market

Lessee

User of an asset owned by someone else under the terms of a lease agreement.

#Contracts

L

Lessor

Owner of an asset used by someone else under the terms of a lease agreement.

#Contracts

Leveraged lease

A lease agreement where the cost of the asset is, in effect, split between the lessor and a third-party lender. The legal owner of the asset is the lessor. The lessor offers the asset as security for a loan from the third-party lender. The lender has restricted recourse to the lessee's income stream and the asset being leased. Leveraged leases are more common in the US.

#Contracts

Lien

A right to retain assets owned by another party until that party has paid money that it owes. Lessors may face difficulties recovering a leased asset if a lien has been created against it. The lien should be 'discharged' once the amounts owed have been paid.

#Risk

Limited company

A privately-owned company, meaning that the shares are not traded on a stock market. A shareholder's liability is limited to the value of the shares that they own but have not paid for. Leasing to limited companies is outside of the scope of FCA regulation of consumer credit.

#Business

Limited Liability Partnership (LLP)

A business owned by its partners, each of whom shares responsibility for the business. An individual partner's liability is limited to the amount they invest in the business.

#Business

L

Line of credit

A flexible borrowing facility allowing the customer to borrow up to a maximum amount over a period of time. The mechanics of a line of credit can apply equally to leasing, e.g. a customer can be guaranteed lease facilities for a total value of assets. One of the arguments for leasing is to help the business to preserve its capacity to borrow if it is getting close to using up its other lines of credit.

#Alternatives

Liquidation

The process of winding up a company. A liquidation can be arranged on either a voluntary or a compulsory basis. A voluntary liquidation can be a creditor's voluntary liquidation, where the owners choose to liquidate the business because it cannot pay its debts, or a members' voluntary liquidation, where the business can settle its remaining debts but the owners wish to close it.

#Risk

Listed company

A public company listed on the London Stock Exchange, including the AIM for smaller growing companies, or another stock exchange.

#Business

Loan to value ratio

Ratio of the amount lent or advance to the actual value of an asset being financed.

#Operations

Long funding lease

L

For corporation tax rules, a lease that is considered by HMRC to be essentially a financing arrangement. It excludes hire purchase. Includes all finance leases longer than 7 years; a finance lease with term between 5 and 7 years meeting certain criteria including a low residual value; and an operating lease with term longer than 5 years meeting certain criteria including the term being more than 65% of the asset's useful life and/or the lease payments being more than 80% of the asset's original value.

The lessee claims the capital allowances for a long funding lease and offsets the interest element of the lease payments against profits. The intention of these complicated rules was to align the tax treatment of longer leases with that of taking out a loan to buy the equipment.

#Tax

Loss Given Default (LGD)

Ratio of the loss due to the default of a borrower to the amount outstanding at default. The LGD for leasing is measured after any benefit obtained from selling the asset is realised. It is reported as a percentage of the exposure at default, the difference between the cashflows received by the lessor and those contracted to be paid.

#Prudential

Maintenance

Lessees will usually be required to service or maintain leased assets to keep them in good condition. The lease might stipulate that the service or maintenance should be carried out by the equipment manufacturer or a firm approved by the manufacturer or lessor.

#Asset #Contracts

Managed Equipment Service (MES)

In the NHS, the outsourcing of the ownership and operation of medical equipment, such as imaging systems for radiology, to a third party. The provider is likely to have contracts with multiple NHS Trusts, enabling it to achieve economies of scale. Where used, MES arrangements mean that the potential lessee is the MES provider, rather than the Trust.

#Public sector

M

Manufacturer buy-back

See Buy-back.

#Asset

Margin

A lessor's profit margin is equal to its spread less its operating expense less its cost of risk.

#Accounting #Operations

Market rental

The lease price that would be agreed by unconnected ('arms-length') lessors and lessees. It is essentially a test of reasonableness that is used in accounting and taxation.

For lease accounting where the lessee has the ability to continue to lease for a secondary period at a rent that is substantially lower than market rent, this is an indicator of a finance lease. This applies to IAS 17 and UK standards, but there is no such concept in IFRS 16.

#Accounting

Master lease

Agreed general terms and conditions between a lessee and lessor to apply to leases which may be taken out or drawn down from time to time. It is supported by a lease schedule that sets out the assets that are leased at any point in time, together with any terms that are specific to those assets. This arrangement is more often used by larger lessees who will need to add to or change their leased assets frequently and do not wish to have to renegotiate the main terms and conditions each time.

#Legal

M

Mezzanine

A form of debt that sits between normal debt and actual equity. Holders rank below senior debt, which has earlier rights of repayment and first rights in a liquidation, but ahead of ordinary shareholders. Higher interest rates generally apply than for senior debt. It may be used by some larger companies to raise finance for major investment projects that may include equipment.

#Alternatives

Middle ticket lease

The industry tends to refer mainly to small ticket business (lower value lease agreements, perhaps less than £50,000) and big-ticket (traditionally more than £20 million). For completeness, middle ticket business covers everything between the two, although it is not a term in such common use and the value ranges are not at all precise.

#Market

Minimum lease payments

The charges to which the lessee is committed under the agreement, including any fees and charges outside of the regular lease rentals. The term is used mainly in lease accounting.

#Accounting

Minimum period lease

A lease that will carry on indefinitely until it is cancelled after a defined minimum hire period. The rental payments will usually remain at the same level and frequency after the minimum period. It tends to be used where there is not expected to be an extension beyond the initial term. Also referred to as an open-ended lease, minimum term rental or infinite rental.

#Products

M

Minimum term

See Primary lease period.

#Contracts

Money laundering

The process of concealing or disguising the proceeds of criminal activity, often by depositing cash into bank accounts in such a way that the money appears to have been obtained legally. See Anti-Money Laundering.

#Regulation

Money market

Wholesale finance markets, dominated by banks. Non-bank lessors may also raise funds by borrowing on this market.

#Funding

Multi financing

Where the same asset is unknowingly funded by more than one lessor. It is a type of fraud that permits lessees (often working with intermediaries) to either embezzle the amounts paid out, or to improperly raise money on a secured basis. The industry is exposed to this type of fraud partly due to the lack of a comprehensive asset register, but lessors can mitigate the risk through asset inspection and secure marking.

#Assets #Risk

National Association of Commercial Finance Brokers (NACFB)

Trade association representing a wide range of business finance brokers, including specialists in commercial mortgages, bridging finance, and invoice finance as well as vehicle and equipment leasing. It was founded in 1992 and the British Leasing Brokers Association was amalgamated in 1996. It is run by an elected Board of Directors supported by the Executive. It promotes high standards through its code of conduct, complaints handling arrangements and educational programmes including a Certificate in Business Banking and Conduct qualification run with the London Institute of Banking and Finance.

In 2018 the NACFB launched its Patrons Charter, which sets out how the Association's Patrons (that include most lessors dealing with brokers) should behave. Among other requirements, Patrons are expected to deal with brokers and clients with the 'utmost good faith and with a standard of competence, fairness and courtesy'. They should also exercise appropriate levels of due diligence when accepting introductions. The Charter appears to be an effort to address concerns that relationships between brokers and funders were sometimes marked by insufficient mutual trust and respect.

www.nacfb.org.uk

#Associations

National Crime Agency

Government department that leads the UK's efforts to cut serious and organised crime. If a lessor had any concerns arising from its anti-money laundering procedures it would file a Suspicious Activity Report (SAR) with the NCA.
www.nationalcrimeagency.gov.uk.

#Risk

National Fraud Intelligence Bureau

Run by the City of London Police, the Bureau aims to identify serial offenders, organised crime gangs and established and emerging crime types. Incidents of fraud are reported using the City of London's Action Fraud centre. There is no legal obligation to report fraud but FCA-authorised firms should have a financial crime policy and this would normally include reporting procedures. Not all cases are investigated; the emphasis is on dealing with underlying problems rather than individual incidents.

N

#Risk

Near-prime

Customers with lower tiered credit ratings or some minor indication of financial difficulty (e.g. occasional missed payments) but not enough to classify as non-prime. The term is more commonly used in the consumer arena than in business lending.

#Credit

Net book value

The value of an asset on a company's balance sheet. It is equal to the original cost of an asset less depreciation and less any permanent decline in the asset's value that has been recognised in the accounts. Also referred to as the carrying value of the asset.

#Accounting

Net investment in the lease

For lease accounting, the lessor's gross investment in a finance lease discounted at the implicit interest rate.

#Accounting

Net present value (NPV)

The value of future cash flows calculated using the Discounted cash flow technique.

For a lessor, NPV would include the initial cost of the equipment, the lease payments, and any sale of the asset at the end of the lease.

For the lessee, the technique can be used as part of a lease vs. purchase analysis. More widely, it is used to assess the case for a new business investment, with a positive net present value for the investment suggesting it will be profitable.

The discount rate used for an NPV calculation is critical. For a lessee assessing an investment it may be the weighted average cost of capital, which takes account of the firm's different sources of capital and their tax treatment.

#Finance

NHS Supply Chain

An outsourced procurement and logistics operation for the National Health Service. Established in 2006 for an initial ten-year period as an agreement between the NHS Business Services Authority (NHSBSA) and DHL Excel Europe Limited. The agreement was extended in 2016 for two years. It established a leasing framework arrangement for six categories of medical and IT assets.

The framework is intended to help hospital trusts obtain good value from leasing with having to complete the normal public procurement steps each time they lease. Use of the framework is optional and an alternative framework is run by University Hospital Southampton Trust in which 12 lessors participate.

New arrangements for the operation of Supply Chain are being implemented by the Department of Health, intended to enable the NHS to make better use of its buying power.

#Public sector

Ninety percent test

For lease accounting, a measure used in the past to help define whether an agreement was an operating lease or finance lease. Under SSAP 21, if the net present value of the minimum lease payments amounted to "substantially all (normally 90 percent or more) of the fair value of the leased asset" this used to indicate that the lease was a finance lease.

#Accounting

Nominal rate

The interest rate including inflation. Where rates are quoted for leasing they are usually stated in nominal terms.

#Finance

N

Non-performing loan

A loan or lease which is in arrears (typically 90 days or more overdue).

#Credit

Non-recourse leasing

Where the lessor is responsible for any losses from a lease agreement. If the agreement was introduced by an equipment vendor, the vendor is not required to purchase the lessor's remaining financial interest in a lease where there has been a default. May also apply where there is an intermediate lessor, and in that situation the head lessor is responsible for any losses.

#Market

Novation

Where one lease agreement is substituted for another with the same terms. The original agreement is extinguished (cancelled) and a new one is created. For example, if a firm is acquired by another, the lessor might be content to cancel the lease in the name of the original lessee and start a new agreement with the acquirer for the remaining term of the original agreement. A fee may be applied for this service. An alternative arrangement is Assignment.

The term can also refer to the novation of the order for an asset. The lessee may contract to purchase an asset from a supplier. This commitment is then transferred from the lessee to the lessor near the time of delivery of the asset.

#Legal

Off-balance sheet

O

Refers to a business's assets and liabilities not being recorded on its balance sheet. Under IAS 17 operating leases are off-balance sheet for the lessee but for IFRS 16 this will change.

#Accounting

Off-lease equipment

Equipment that has been returned to the lessor to dispose of. It is often sold by an agent or sold at auction. It may also be returned to the manufacturer or supplier if there is a buy-back provision in place. Alternatively, some lease agreements allow the lessee to sell the equipment as the lessor's agent at the end of the lease and to then receive a rebate of rentals based on a percentage of the sale price. Also referred to as 'ex-lease equipment'.

#Assets

Open banking

To increase competition in the retail banking markets since the financial crisis in 2008, successive governments have looked at ways of allowing new entrants to access data on individual consumer and business accounts. The largest nine current account providers must now allow regulated businesses access to a customer's financial data. Arrangements are in place for the data to be shared securely with authorised third-parties.

This is intended to create new opportunities for non-bank lessors. It is seen as helping to overcome an information disadvantage compared to current account providers that have access to the detailed current account data.

Data is only available for sharing if current account holders give their consent. It is not yet clear how many SMEs would agree to do so, whether those that do would include firms that could be helped using leasing, or indeed whether the data in the current account will provide a reliable basis for assessing credit risk.

#Business #Credit

Open-ended lease

See Minimum period lease.

#Products

Operating lease

A lease where the lessor retains the risks and rewards of owning the asset. According to IAS 17 indicators that a lease is an operating rather than finance lease include the lease term being for less than a major part of the economic life of the asset, the lessee not having any option to purchase or a bargain purchase option, and the present value of the lease payments being less than the value of the asset.

For UK tax, the lessor is eligible for capital allowances unless the lease is caught by the long-funding lease rules. If the lease is for more than 5 years, term is more than 65% of the asset's useful life and/or the lease payments are more than 80% of the asset's original value then the lessee is eligible for allowances.

#Accounting #Products #Tax

Operating profit/loss

The difference between the operating revenue of a firm and the costs involved in earning that revenue.

Operating revenue for lessors is often the same as total Revenue, including finance income for finance leases and operating lease rentals. Revenue from associated services provided, such as maintenance, will be added, but the timing will be subject to accounting revenue recognition rules. Nonrecurring items, such as the sale of an office or accounting adjustments, are excluded from operating revenue.

Operating costs include depreciation for equipment on operating leases, marketing and administration, and the overheads of the business. Indirect costs of lease contracts, such as commissions and legal fees, can be amortised over the lease term.

Lessors vary in how they report interest expense. Some present net interest (revenue less interest expense) as their revenue and exclude interest from operating cost. Others report their interest expense under the operating cost heading.

Lessors may also choose whether to offset provisions for losses against their revenue, or to set these out separately as an operating cost.

#Accounting

Operational risk

For regulatory (FCA and PRA) purposes, the risk of loss resulting from inadequate or failed internal procedures, human error, failures in internal systems, or external events.

Operational exposure is the degree of operational risk faced by a firm. It is measured based on the likelihood and impact of a particular type of operational loss occurring.

Operational risk profile describes the types of operational risks that it faces. The FCA specifies that risk to the quality of service provided to customers should be considered alongside the direct risk exposures of the firm. Operational risk is separate from the risks most often associated with leasing contracts, being credit and asset risks. The regulators' focus on operational risk provides

a useful reminder that lessors should maintain a wide perspective
in their risk management activities.

#Risk #Prudential

Option

A contractual right, but not an obligation. For leasing a lessee
might have the option to extend a lease for a defined period and
at a defined rate, or to buy or sell an asset. The option will be set
out in the lease agreement.

#Contracts

Option to purchase

See Bargain purchase option.

#Contracts

Outsourcing

Contracting business processes to a third party. A common use
of outsourcing providers in the leasing industry is to take over a
portfolio of leases from a business that is leaving the market. Some
lessors also focus on new business and leave back-office contract
administration and collections to a third-party. Outsourcers may
also act as a standby servicer for securitisations.

#Operations

Origination

The term used in the leasing industry instead of 'sales' or 'new
business'. All new leases are originated, either through direct
sales activity or through intermediaries including brokers and
suppliers.

#Operations

Overcollateralisation

Where a borrower provides security in excess of the debt
outstanding, protecting the lender from a fall in the value of the

security. Over-collaterisation may be used to help sell asset-backed securities.

#Funding

Own-book

Where asset finance brokers decide to fund some deals themselves using their own capital or borrowed funds. They may select the better deals but sometimes will use their own-book to help customers well-known to them who might otherwise not be able to raise finance. The own-book may use block financing.

#Intermediaries

Partial exemption

Because the regular payments for hire purchase agreements are exempt for VAT there is a complication for lessors concerning how much of the VAT they incur on providing hire purchase can be recovered. VAT on the purchased asset is recoverable, but the question is how much VAT on the lessor's other costs, or 'overheads', should be recoverable. A business with both taxable and exempt supplies is considered partially exempt, and will not be able to recover all of the VAT on its overheads.

Between 1984 and 2000 the leasing industry had an agreement with HMRC which allowed a 15% recovery of VAT incurred on overheads related to Hire Purchase. This agreement eventually fell apart as many in the industry believed the rate to be too low.

Following a series of tribunal and court cases over many years led by Volkswagen Financial Services, during which the industry called for a higher recovery rate, the Court of Appeal concluded in 2015 that the rate should not be zero percent as HMRC had argued. HMRC's logic was that lessor's overheads are incurred only in providing the financial service, which is the non-taxable supply, and therefore are not recoverable at all. The case is expected to be taken to the Supreme Court.

If the 'right' answer is not zero, the difficult question remains of what the figure should be, as any allocation of an overhead is always going to be a judgement. It may be that a new compromise will eventually be found between HMRC and the industry. In the meantime, lessors are left having to deal with considerable uncertainty that has already persisted for over a decade.

#Tax

Partnership

A business owned by its partners, each of whom shares responsibility for the business. There is joint and several liability, meaning that each partner is potentially liable for the entire debt of the business.

#Business

Payment frequency

Lease payments may be agreed at any frequency but are usually monthly or quarterly. The frequency is a trade-off between smoothing cash-flow for the lessee and minimising administration costs for both lessee and lessor. Each payment may be due at the start of the period ('payment in advance') or the end ('payment in arrears').

#Contracts

P

Payment Card Industry Data Security Standard (PCI DSS)

PCI DSS is the worldwide Payment Card Industry Data Security Standard that was set up to help businesses process card payments securely and reduce card fraud. In general, lessors rely on direct debit or bank transfers for payment, but some may accept card payments from consumers or small businesses for rental payments.

#Operations

Payout

The point in the process of setting up a new lease where the lessor pays the supplier of the equipment. It is also usually the point when the documentation is signed off, or ratified, such that the lease starts and the parties are fully committed to the arrangement. A key anti-fraud check her, is that the payment is made to the correct bank account.

#Risk #Operations

Peer-to-peer finance

See Alternative finance.

#Alternatives

Penetration rate

The proportion of equipment sold by a manufacturer or dealer for which lease finance is arranged. The term is more frequently used in consumer finance, e.g. for cars, but is equally relevant for business finance. The FLA reports lease penetration rates as a proportion of total investment by UK businesses in machinery, equipment and purchased software. The long-term penetration rate is around 30% but in recent years has been as high as 34%.

#Market

P

Peppercorn rent/rentals

Agreed lease payments that would be due in a secondary or extension period if they have been set at a nominal amount. Peppercorn rents/rentals are used to support the lessor/lessee relationship and to preserve the tax position.

#Contracts

Personal guarantee

It is common for smaller ticket asset finance agreements with small businesses that directors are asked to sign a personal guarantee. This can enable lessors to fund equipment that would otherwise be declined. In the event of the business not being able to pay the amounts which fall due, these then become the responsibility of the guarantor, who has to clear any arrears and fees and then maintain future payments as and when they fall due. If a guarantee is given by a director, they are sometimes referred to as a director's guarantee, or 'DG'. If it is given by an individual who has an interest in the underlying agreement, it is referred to as a personal guarantee, or 'PG'.

To satisfy legal requirements, it is important to ensure that the guarantor has given informed consent and that they have not been subjected to any undue influence in signing the guarantee. Whilst directors are often assumed to have an interest in 'guaranteeing their business', this is especially important for guarantors who are not directors and funders need to take steps to demonstrate that they have taken appropriate steps to ensure that independent legal advice has been recommended or obtained.

Capping the maximum liability is sometimes permitted by funders, and personal guarantee Insurance products are available. This is often used alongside an Indemnity.

#Contracts #Credit

Place of supply

For VAT purposes, the location where an asset is delivered by the supplier. The place of supply for cross-border leases will determine where VAT will be paid on the asset purchase by the lessor. The rules for the supply of services are more complicated. For transportation assets, the place of supply will be where the customer is based, rather than where the asset is used.

#Taxation

Plant and machinery

For corporate tax, investment in plant and machinery is eligible for capital allowances. HMRC helpfully defines machinery as being machines with moving parts. It includes computers and other electronic devices. Plant is anything that is used in a business but is neither part of the business premises nor an item of stock. This becomes relevant to lessors for equipment such as lighting and heating; see Fixtures.

#Taxation

Politically Exposed Persons (PEPs) Checks

Individuals whose prominent position in public life may make them vulnerable to corruption. The full definition of a PEP is set out in the Money Laundering, Terrorist Financing and Transfer of Funds (Information on the Payer) Regulations 2017. The scope includes immediate family members and known close associates of these individuals. Credit reference agencies offer tools to help identify PEPs.

Like all other financial institutions, lessors are expected to undertake enhanced anti money-laundering (AML) checks with dealing with PEPs or companies they are associated with. The involvement of a PEP is unlikely, however, to increase the actual risk of a lessee, and will often bring benefits from the individual's experience and good-standing in the business community.

#Regulation

Portfolio

P

A collection of finance agreements held by a lessor. May also be used to refer to the total outstanding receivables owed to a lessor.

For IFRS 16, lessees may combine a portfolio of lease contracts with similar characteristics (for example, similar assets and similar remaining lease term) to simplify reporting.

#Market

Present value

The value of a future payment or a series of future payments, discounted at an interest rate. See Net Present Value.

#Finance

Primary lease period

The agreed minimum term of the lease. It should be in line with the expected useful life of the equipment to the lessee's business.

#Contracts

Prime

The most credit-worthy customers that a lessor can deal with. Tends to refer to businesses with no indication of financial difficulties, although precise definitions vary between firms. It can also refer more generally to leases of Hard assets. More commonly used in consumer than business lending. Other customers may be Near Prime or Sub Prime.

#Credit

Principal

The sum on which interest is charged or fees and charges levied.

#Contract

Private equity

Investment in firms that are not publicly listed. The term tends to refer to specialist investment management firms that manage funds that invest in other firms. A small number of private equity firms, including Cabot Investment Management and Star Capital, have been active in recent years in the UK buying asset finance brokers and lenders. The firms bring experience and their expertise to the sector, although they typically expect high returns.

#Funding

P

Probability of Default (PD)

The likelihood that a lessee will not pay all if its contracted lease payments. Research by Leaseurope published in 2013 found that the average probability of default for leasing is lower than that for other types of business lending. Default rates are low because the leased assets are often critical to the business and for this reason paying the lease is often prioritised over other debts.

1-year probability of default (1-year PD) is the probability of a default event occurring in the next 12 months. Lifetime probability of default is the probability of a default event over the remaining period of the lease contract.

#Prudential

Professionalism

There has been much debate about what professionalism in financial services means and how to achieve it. At one level it is about day-to-day conduct of business, including treating customers with respect, transparency and making ethical judgements. Above that, the Banking Standards Board notes, it is about culture, behaviour and competence in firms and across the industry. Many of the leasing industry's trade associations and other bodies aim to promote professionalism.

#Business

Profile

The pattern of lease payments over the period of the lease. For a 3+33 profile, for example, the lessee's first payment is the equivalent of the amount normally paid over three months, and this is followed by 33 normal monthly payments. Hence if a normal monthly rate is £100, the initial rental will be £300, followed by 33 months of £100 payments.

#Contracts

Profitability

There are several accounting measures of profitability. The most common is probably Profit Before Interest and Tax (PBIT). Other options include Earnings before Interest, Taxes, Depreciation and Amortisation (EBITDA) and Profit Before Tax (PBT).

A quirk of the new international accounting standard, IFRS 16, is that it will increase PBIT and EBITDA measures for lessees that use today's operating leases. At present the entire cost of the lease is an operating expense. Under IFRS 16 the interest element of the lease expense will fall outside of these measures.

#Accounting

Promissory Note

A written commitment to make a payment. Occasionally a lessee will provide a series of such notes rather than sign a direct debit or standing order.

#Legal

Project finance

A lending arrangement for a specific, and usually major, capital infrastructure projects, such as a building or road. Security is typically provided by the cash flows that the project is expected to generate, such as rentals or tolls. Part of the lending may be structured as a lease.

#Business

Proposal

A presentation of a customer's funding needs in detail (often supplied by a dealer or finance broker) which gets entered into a funders' system for a credit review and subsequent underwriting decision.

P

#Contract

Provision

An adjustment made to the lessor's accounts to recognise or anticipate that lessees in arrears will default. The amount provided for reduces shareholders' funds and is shown as a liability on the balance sheet. There are two main methods of provisioning: the lessor might assess each individual receivable for larger agreements and make specific provisions; or for smaller transactions the lessor will maintain a general provision at an appropriate percentage of the value of a relevant portfolio of leases based on age of debt.

#Accounting

Prudential regulation

Standards set for banks and other financial institutions aimed at protecting the stability of the financial system. The Standards require the institutions to control risks and hold adequate capital.

In general, deposit taking banks are prudentially regulated, whereas non-bank lessors are not. It can be argued this gives the non-banks an advantage, but a benefit of the regulation for banks is that it enables them to raise capital for lending at a lower rate than is likely to be available to the non-banks.

#Prudential

Public Liability Company (PLC)

The legal form for a company that issues shares to the public and has limited liability.

Many of the UK's largest companies are PLCs. Research looking at the use of leasing by the FTSE 350 (the top 350 companies by market capitalisation) in 2010 found that these companies leased only a small proportion of their business equipment, although use of leasing varied considerably between companies. To some extent this will reflect the availability of low cost finance for many listed companies.

Listed companies are Public Interest Entities under European law (whilst the UK is part of the European Union). As such they must use international accounting rules including, in due course, the new lease accounting standard, IFRS 16.

#Business

Purchase option

A contractual right, but not an obligation, for the lessee to purchase the leased assets at the end of the lease term. If there is a purchase option, the agreement is one of credit and not hire.

#Contracts

Purchase price

The price paid for the asset to be leased. It is usually agreed between the supplier and the lessee without the involvement of the lessor. The lessor will want to check that the price paid is reasonable, as if not the asset will provide inadequate security.

Lessors may use external services, including those provided by chartered surveyors and specialist providers, to help confirm the reasonableness of prices paid.

#Asset

Put option

Where the lessor has the right to resell the equipment to the broker, supplier or another party at a specified price, either at the end of the agreement or in the event of the equipment being repossessed following a default.

#Asset

Rate

The interest rate on which the lease payments are based. It is often expressed as a 'Rate per £1,000'. The Rate per £1,000 is multiplied by the cost of the equipment less the deposit to give the monthly rental.

#Finance

R

Ratio analysis

The financial assessment of a company by calculating ratios from figures in the financial accounts and comparing them with previous periods or other companies. See Cost/income, Cost of risk, Return on capital employed, Return on assets, Return on equity, Loan to value ratio.

#Operations

Real interest rate

The interest rate adjusted to remove the effects of inflation.

#Finance

Rear-end loading

A lease payments Profile where larger payments, such as Balloon payments, are made towards the end of the contracted period.

#Contracts

Receivables

The lease payments due to a lessor.

#Credit

Recession

Downturn in economic activity where the UK Gross Domestic Product declines for two successive quarters. Business equipment leasing is often seen as a leading indicator of a recession, as investment in new equipment declines due to business uncertainty about the future. The leasing market lost around one-third of its total volume in the recession that started in 2008, and on an inflation-adjusted basis took around eight years to recover.

#Business

Recourse leasing

Where an equipment vendor agrees to meet certain obligations in the event of the lessee defaulting. The vendor might purchase the lessor's remaining financial interest in a lease by making the lessee's payments for the remaining duration of the lease or for a limited period. Alternatively, the vendor might agree to repurchase the equipment from the lessor or to sell it on behalf of the lessor.

#Market

Reducing balance depreciation

A pattern of depreciation where depreciation is calculated as a constant percentage of the original cost of the fixed asset less the expected residual value at the start of the lease and less the accumulated depreciation to date. The main alternative is Straight-line depreciation.

#Accounting

Refinancing

Replacing an existing finance agreement with another for the same equipment. This may be done to extend the term of a lease, thereby reducing the repayment amounts. See also Roll-over.

#Contracts

Regional Growth Fund

Launched in 2010, the Fund invested £2.7 billion to help local businesses grow and take on more staff across England. Several lessors participated in the Fund and were able to offer lessees Government subsidies towards their deposits on new assets. To be eligible businesses needed to show that the investment would create or safeguard jobs and would otherwise not take place. The final round of schemes using the Fund were approved in in 2015.

#Market

R

Regulated agreement

A lease agreement regulated under consumer credit law. To be regulated, it needs to be a non-exempt agreement with an individual, an unincorporated business, or a partnership with 2 or 3 partners that is not a limited liability partnership.

#Conduct

Regulatory capital

The capital a bank is required by regulators to keep. See Capital adequacy.

#Prudential

Rejection

Decline of a leasing application or proposal because of poor credit history, unsuitable asset, or another reason. Small businesses may be offered support under the Bank Referral Scheme.

#Credit

Relationship lending

Where a lessor aims to build such a strong partnership with a client that they become the default lessor for any equipment the business requires. It brings obvious benefits to both the lessor and lessee but is difficult to achieve. Many of the most successful asset finance brokers have a relationship of this sort with their clients.

#Market

R

Remarketing agreement

An agreement by a Supplier to resell equipment at the end of a lease. This might be part of a Dealer recourse guarantee, or simply a standard arrangement for the end of lease agreements. The arrangement may incentivise the Supplier to achieve a high price by giving them a share of the proceeds. For the lessor, it can often achieve a higher price than selling the equipment at auction. A more definite alternative is a Repurchase agreement.

#Intermediaries

Renewables

Equipment associated with the use of natural resources, such as solar or wind energy.

#Market

Renewal option

Where the lessee can choose to extend the lease term for a defined period and at a pre-agreed cost. If there is no renewal option it is the lessor who has the choice at the end of the minimum lease period of whether to offer an extension and on what terms.

#Contracts

Rentals

The regular amounts paid by the lessee to the lessor during the term of the lease agreement. May also be referred to as lease payments, although lease payments would also include any fees or other additional charges.

#Contracts

Repossession

Where the lessor recovers its leased asset following the lessee failing to meet the terms of the lease contract by falling into default. Any value in the equipment can help mitigate the loss due to the customer's indebtedness.

#Asset #Risk

R

Repurchase agreement

An agreement by a Supplier to buy back equipment from the lessor at the end of a lease. This might be part of a Dealer recourse guarantee, or simply a standard arrangement for the end of lease agreements. The arrangement gives the Supplier any benefits from achieving a higher price. A softer alternative is a Remarketing agreement.

#Intermediaries

Repudiation

Where it is clear that a lessee does not intend, or is unable, to meet its future obligations under the lease agreement, this may amount to a repudiation, or breach, of the agreement. Evidence of repudiation may permit the lessor to repossess the leased equipment and to terminate the agreement.

#Legal

Reseller

Firms, other than manufacturers, that sell vehicles or equipment to businesses or individuals. A Reseller may be exclusively appointed by a manufacturer or distributor or may sell the products of various manufacturers or distributors. Most Resellers add further solutions or services making them a 'Value Added' Reseller (VAR). The term is typically used in the IT sector. See also Dealer.

#Intermediaries

Residual risk

The possibility that the lessor will be unable to sell the asset at the end of the lease agreement at the price factored into the lease, or that the lessor is unable to remarket the asset if that had been planned.

#Risk

R

Residual value

The market value of an asset at the end of the lease. The value can be guaranteed by a third party, or more usually, unguaranteed. Equipment may have residual value even if it has been fully depreciated for accounting purposes and fully amortised under the terms of the lease agreement.

#Assets

Residual value insurance

An insurance policy that covers the risk of the asset needing to be sold by a lessor at the end of a lease for less than the insured value. Tends to be used only for high value equipment with substantial secondary market values such as aircraft, boats, construction and medical equipment.

#Assets #Risk

Residual value guarantee

A guarantee made to a lessor that the value of an asset at the end of a lease will be at least a certain amount. The guarantee may be made by an insurer in return for a premium or by another party, for example a dealer or manufacturer. Residual value insurance from third-party insurers was commonly found in the 1970s and early 1980s. Following tax changes and higher than expected claims it is now quite unusual.

#Assets #Risk

Restrictive covenant

A term in the agreement that restricts the actions of a party. See Covenant.

#Contracts

Retail bank

R

According to the FCA, banks that accept deposits from individuals, 'micro-enterprises' (up to 10 employees, turnover under €2million and €2 million balance sheet) and charities, operate accounts for those customers and provide associated services. More generally, a bank that operates consumer and business current accounts.

#Market

Retention

See Holdback.

Retention of title

Suppliers often seek to retain clear title until the equipment is fully paid-for, and do so by inserting a clause to this effect on their invoice. This arrangement is not commonly considered to be a lease, although it shares many of the characteristics of leasing.

#Legal

Return on assets

Net profit before tax as a percentage of the average portfolio size over a period. The Leaseurope Index showed a weighted average return on assets of 1.8% in 2017.

#Operations

Return conditions

The terms of the lease concerning the condition in which leased equipment should be returned and the logistical arrangements for its return including who will arrange any de-installation, transportation and storage.

#Assets #Contracts

Return on capital employed

Operating profit divided by capital employed. Leasing assets compared to buying can increase the ratio for lessees, as under IAS 17 operating leases are not included in capital employed at all, and for finance leases the capital amount may be lower than for an equivalent owned asset. This effect is removed by IFRS 16.

#Accounting

Return on equity

In general use, net profit before tax divided by shareholders' funds or the company's net worth. For bank-owned lessors it may be necessary to estimate the shareholders' funds dedicated to the leasing product.

#Operations

Revenue

For lease accounting, the lessor calculates revenue separately for finance leases and operating leases. For finance leases, the lessor reports the finance income. The revenue is usually higher towards the beginning of the lease as that is when the lessor's investment in the lease is at its highest, i.e. as the lessee has only started to repay the principal. For operating leases, the full income from the lessee is reported as revenue usually on a straight-line basis, i.e. the same amount each period.

#Accounting

Revolving credit

A flexible loan that allows the borrower to repay and then borrow again up to a defined limit. It is used for stock finance, a form of asset based lending.

#Alternatives

Right-of-use (ROU) asset

According to the International Accounting Standards Board (IASB), an asset is "a resource controlled by the entity as a result of past events and from which future economic benefits are expected to flow to the entity". Based on this the IASB concluded for the new accounting standard IFRS 16 that leasing always creates an asset for the lessee, termed the ROU asset. Its value is calculated based principally on the contracted lease payments over the remaining period of the lease term.

R

#Accounting

Risk weighted assets

See Capital adequacy.

#Prudential

Roll-over

Where an existing lease agreement is terminated early, and the value of the outstanding payments is added to a new lease. It means that the value of the new lease will exceed the asset value.

In the right circumstances this can help the lessee, allowing a business whose needs have changed unexpectedly to obtain more appropriate equipment without having to make a lump sum payment. Unfortunately, roll-overs can also leave less sophisticated lessees facing high rentals that exceed the benefits they obtain from the equipment they are leasing.

#Contracts

Rolling Stock Operating Company (ROSCO)

ROSCOs own most of the coaches, locomotives and freight wagons that are run by the UK's train operating and freight operating companies. As the passenger operating companies are awarded franchises for routes for periods well below the useful life of most rolling stock, operating leases are used.

Three ROSCOs were set up in 1994 at the time of the privatisation of British Rail. This proved controversial when the newly privatised companies were subsequently resold within a few years at much higher prices. A review by the Competition Commission (now the Competition and Markets Authority) which reported in 2009 found problems with competition in the train leasing market due to the limited choice of stock available to the operating companies.

The largest ROSCOs are Angel Trains, Evershot Rail Group and Porterbook Leasing Company. The value of their combined leases to the operating companies in 2015 was £2.2 billion.

#Market

Rule of 78

See Sum of the digits.

#Accounting

Run-off

Where a lessor has ceased writing new business, their existing portfolio is said to be in 'runoff'. In this situation some lessors might choose to either sell the book of receivables to a third-party or outsource the lease management. Others will continue with an (increasingly) skeleton staff until the time comes to 'turn the lights off'.

#Operations

Salary sacrifice

An agreement between an employer and an employee to reduce the employee's salary in return for a corresponding benefit, which may include a 'company' car or a personally leased car through an arrangement made by the employer. The arrangements can lead to tax savings for both employee and employer. The Government is reviewing the rules and this may lead to the tax advantages for salary sacrifice cars being removed.

#Tax

Sale and leaseback

Arrangement whereby a company sells some of its assets to a lessor for a lump sum and leases the assets back. The company frees up cash whilst retaining use of the assets. May be referred to as Sale and HP-back.

#Products

Sales-aid

A finance programme set up by a supplier or manufacturer to support the sales of their products, sometimes through a third party funder but sometimes through their own captive finance company.

The documentation may sometimes be drawn up in the name of the supplier, who will then act as the agent of the lessor. The supplier may sometimes also be responsible for collecting the lease payments and passing the lease element across to the lessor. This can be useful when the supplier is also providing other services, such as maintenance, and wishes to issue bundled invoices.

It is important to meet FCA disclosure requirements for regulated agreements and also HMRC rules for the VAT treatment of invoices that combine leases with associated services.

#Market

Salvage value

Estimate of the minimum value for a recovered leased asset. Unlike the residual value, it assumes the asset will not be in a saleable or recondition-able condition. In many cases, the assumption may be made that the savage value is zero, as it is net of recovery costs.

#Assets

Sanctions checks

Financial sanctions orders may prohibit any financial services being provided to designated individuals, organisations, governments or countries. The FCA expects regulated firms to adhere to these sanctions.

HM Treasury maintains a list of sanctions for UK individuals and organisations. Other governments, regulators and law enforcement agencies also publish sanctions that will require consideration in order to mitigate the risk of financial crime. Many lessors use their credit reference agency to check for any possible matches, however unlikely these are.

#Regulation

Schedule

A detailed list of the assets that are being leased which accompanies a Master Lease agreement.

#Contracts

SECCI

Standard European Consumer Credit Information, a standardised sheet of summary information about the lease agreement that lessors must provide to customers before they sign a regulated consumer credit agreement.

#Conduct

Secondary market

The buying and selling of rights to existing leases or portfolios of lease outside of a securitisation structure. Secondary market transactions can help lessors to manage their exposures to individual companies or sectors. In the UK there is only a very limited secondary market, mostly transacted between a small number of the larger lessors. In the US is it more usual to find finance companies and investors buying rights to leases.

#Funding

Secondary period

The period of use after the Primary lease period. Some leases allow the lessee to continue using the asset at a 'Peppercorn' rental, payable annually in advance. However, others use a Minimum term agreement and will continue charging rentals at the same rate and frequency.

#Contracts

S

Section 75 claim

Under Section 75 of the Consumer Credit Act 1974, for regulated credit agreements the lessor is jointly and severally liable with the equipment supplier for misrepresentation or breach of contract by the supplier. With a suitable agreement in place, lessors will pass any claims to the supplier to deal with, but if the supplier goes out of business this can leave the lessor exposed.

#Regulation #Risk

Securitisation

The process of issuing Asset-Backed Securities (ABS). The parties involved in securitisation are the originator, sponsor, trustee and investor. The originator brings the assets (e.g. leases) that are to be securitised. The sponsor, typically a bank, may underwrite the performance of the ABS, and may combine assets from a range of lessors into a single ABS issue (termed an Asset Backed Commercial Paper conduit). The trustee administers the trust or special purpose vehicle that will hold the assets. Securitisation is used by some larger lenders, particularly car lessors, to raise funds for further lending.

#Funding

Security

In general, the assets being financed act as the security for a lease. However, in addition, lessors may require personal security of one or more director or owner of the business through a Personal guarantee. Other forms of additional security may also be sought.

#Contracts #Risk

Security deposit

S

Separate from the Deposit that reduces the amount being funded, a Security deposit forms security for the performance of all the lessee's obligations under the lease agreement. At the end of the agreement, it is repaid to the lessee once the equipment is returned in the condition agreed in the contract. Security deposits are uncommon in the UK.

#Contracts #Risk

Self-billing

Leasing agreements sometimes allow for the lessor to collect maintenance payments as the agent of the supplier. This simplifies matters for the lessee by having to make only a single payment. The lessor will then need to receive VAT invoices from the supplier for the amounts collected on its behalf. With the permission of the supplier and HMRC, the lessor can raise these VAT invoices itself, through 'self-billing'.

#Tax

Self-regulation

Where an industry tries to control its own activities to avoid the need for government intervention through independent regulators or changes to the law. The leasing industry's various codes of conduct, including those of the FLA, BVRLA and NACFB, are all forms of self-regulation.

Like most self-regulation, the industry's Codes have had mixed success. They can be credited with having maintained high standards and the reputation of the industry. Compliance with them is, however, voluntary (firms may choose not to join the relevant associations) and often difficult to enforce (expulsion of a member from a trade association for non-compliance is rare).

Many areas covered by the leasing industry's Codes are also now within the scope of the FCA handbook or the (voluntary but independently run) Lending Standards Board's Asset Finance Standards for business customers.

#Regulation

Service

S

For lease accounting, an arrangement where the customer does not direct and control the use of the equipment.

It can be difficult to differentiate a service from a lease. Equipment within a printing facility within a large company might be classified as either a lease or a service. If the machines are operated by the company itself, they are likely to be a lease for accounting purposes.

If the machines are operated by a third party, they are likely to be part of a service, such as Managed Equipment Services in the NHS.

#Accounting

Settlement

See Early settlement.

#Contracts

Shadow banking

The provision of credit by entities that are not banks and therefore are not subject to prudential bank regulation. Up to 30% of total credit is provided by the shadow banking sector, which in its broadest sense encompasses all non-bank lessors.

Shadow banking has been the focus of much work by policy makers and regulators since the economic crisis. It was seen as a primary cause of many of the problems, especially in the US. The main response has been the tightening of prudential rules relevant to banks' lending to non-bank financial institutions.

Further oversight and regulation of 'systematically important' shadow banks is planned. The only lessor categorised under US definitions for this treatment was GE Capital, but GE's status was reviewed in 2016 following its downsizing and its designation was rescinded.

#Regulation

S Shariah leasing

Under Islamic law, financial intermediation advocates the norm of 'risk and profit sharing' in business enterprise. It encourages investment in real economic activities that are asset-based and prohibits pre-determined rates of interest.

Shariah leasing, Ijara, includes Operating Ijara, an operating lease with rental payments and no transfer of ownership, and Ijara Muntahia Bittamleek, where there is a separate contract concerning a transfer of ownership at the end of a lease. The lessor retains responsibility for the leased asset, including insurance and maintenance, during the lease.

#Market

Sharing economy

There is a growing trend in the economy away from buying and owning assets towards paying for temporary access to assets. It is now common to find schemes in consumer markets for the sharing of both tangible assets (bike and car sharing, Airbnb, etc.) and intangible (Spotify, etc.). The outcome is referred to as the new 'sharing economy'.

It could be argued this is nothing new for asset finance. Equipment rental providers have always offered temporary access to assets they have often themselves leased.

As the sharing economy grows in importance in the consumer sector, it is possible that more businesses as well as consumers will stop buying assets outright. This could benefit the existing leasing market, although lessors – perhaps in conjunction with equipment manufacturers and suppliers – may need to innovate and accept great residual value asset risk in order to provide more flexible ways of providing access to assets.

#Business

Short lease

For corporation tax, any lease that is not a long funding lease. This includes any lease with a term of 5 years or less, and a finance lease with a term of 5 to 7 years meeting certain criteria, including the residual value being above 5% of the original value. The lessor claims the capital allowances for a short lease.

#Tax

Short-term lease

For IFRS 16, a lease with a term of 12 months or less, including the effect of any extension options that might be exercised. Such contracts are still classified as leases and are within the scope of the Standard, but lessees may choose not to report them as Right-of-use assets. A summary of short-term leases is instead required in the notes to the accounts.

#Accounting

Side-letter

Where a commitment to a lessee is made outside of the lease
agreement. The commitment might be made by an intermediary
broker or equipment supplier. There is a major risk factor for
lessors if the supplier 'sweetens' a leasing deal by offering extra
benefits without the lessor's knowledge. If the provider of the
side-letter then fails to provide those benefits, whether because the
intention was fraudulent from the outset or because the supplier
has become insolvent, the risk of a default on the lease payments
will increase and there can also be reputational harm.

Anti-fraud checks by the lessor, including calling customers to
check what they have been promised by suppliers, can mitigate
the risk.

In 2012 it was reported that schools had been promised free
laptop computers by the supplier when they leased photocopiers.
Lessors were not aware and the supplier did not deliver the laptops.
The fraud was reported in the national media including on a BBC
Panorama programme entitled 'Reading, Writing and Rip-offs'.
Several large lessors were involved. Most of the schools were fully
compensated by the lessors well before the media coverage.

#Risk

S   Small and Medium-Sized Enterprises (SMEs)

Usually refers to businesses with up to 250 employees. The
Government's more precise definition is a firm with fewer than
250 employees, and either turnover of less than £25m or gross
assets of less than £12.5m. The term encompasses micro-businesses
having up to nine employees, small businesses having ten to 49
employees, and medium-sized businesses having between 50 and
249 employees.

There are 5.7 million SMEs in the UK, more than 99% of all
businesses. They provide 16.1 million jobs, 60% of all private
sector employment in the UK. Around 60% of all UK leasing
by value is with SMEs. Excluding big ticket and fleet leases, the
proportion is likely to be closer to 80%,

#Business

Small ticket lease

Agreements for smaller assets or for smaller total values, perhaps up to £50,000. It can be uneconomic for lessors to deal with customers for small ticket deals, so they are often handled through brokers or suppliers, or possibly online.

#Market

Social responsibility

The ethical principle that suggests businesses should be run to benefit society and not only to maximise the returns to their owners. Lessors' corporate social responsibility programmes might include promoting the use of more environmentally-friendly equipment or helping to support the growth of very small businesses by offering preferential terms.

#Business

Soft assets

Assets that do not meet some or all the DIMS (Durable, Identifiable, Moveable and Saleable) criteria.

#Assets

S

Soft costs

Miscellaneous expenses associated with an investment in assets to be leased that may be bundled into a lease agreement. Examples include delivery and installation costs. Most lessors will be content to include a low level of soft costs in the lease.

#Contract

Soft loan

Loan at a subsidised rate of interest, such as a zero percent finance lease.

#Market

Software

Providing a lease for software is not straightforward, as it is an intangible asset and one that is not licensed by the supplier rather than sold.

An option for lessors is to treat the software element of an investment as a soft asset, for example they may fund an element of software as part of an equipment investment.

Alternatively, the lessor may be able to agree with the software supplier for the lessee's licence agreement to be novated, or transferred, from the lessee to the lessor. In this way, specialist software lessors can finance software on a standalone basis.

Software providers may also offer a 'Software as a Service' (SaaS) solution. Although not presented as such, SaaS has the characteristics of leasing.

#Market

Special purpose vehicle

A legal entity established to facilitate a specific purpose. For a lessor this might be the securitisation of an asset finance portfolio. For a lessee, it might be to operate a specific project, for example to build and operate a wind turbine and claim relevant grants.

#Business #Funding

S

Spread

The difference between the lessor's cost of funds and the interest rate on a lease offered to a lessee.

#Finance

SSAP 21

The UK Statement of Standard Accounting Practice (accounting standard) for leases, issued by the Accounting Standards Committee, predecessor of the Accounting Standards Board, in 1984. SSAP 21 required leased assets under finance leases to be reported on the lessee's balance sheet for the first time. SSAP 21 was superseded in 2015 by FRS 102.

#Accounting

Stage payment

For more complex leases, typically involving a number of assets that require installation work, the lease agreement may stipulate that the lessor will release payments to the equipment supplier following certain events or stages of the project.

#Contract

Standardised Approach

For prudential regulation, the default method by which banks calculate their Risk Weighted Assets. Standard risk weightings are defined by the regulator, the Prudential Regulation Authority. For corporate loans and leases, the Corporate risk weightings vary from 20% to 150% according to the credit rating of the borrower or lessee. An unrated business has a risk weight of 100%. SME loans and leases are risk weighted at either 75% or 85%, a measure intended to promote lending to small businesses.

Compared to the alternative Advanced Internal Ratings Based Approach (AIRB), the Standardised Approach is simple and requires less data to operate. It fails, however, to recognise the relatively low risk nature of leasing. This has two consequences. First, within the bank, the benefits of offering leasing compared to other types of loan will be less significant. Second, banks using the Standardised Approach may find it more difficult to compete with larger banks using the AIRB for corporate customers with strong credit ratings, or where the bank's AIRB models are used to attach a preferential risk weight to leases.

Standby operator

When a lessor sells a portfolio of receivables but continues to manage the agreements on behalf of the buyer, the sale agreement will often require an independent third-party to be appointed.

This firm could, if needed, take over the management of the portfolio.

#Prudential

Standing order

A regular, fixed payment from a bank account. It can be set up by a lessee to make lease payments. Direct debits are more commonly used for smaller agreements.

#Credit

Start-up

A new business, generally one less than three years old. A challenge for a lender is that the business will not have an established credit history. Firms may be eligible for support from the Start-Up Loan Company, part of the Department for Business, Energy and Industrial Strategy.

#Business

Statutory demand

A formal request for payment of a debt owed by an individual or company. When the individual or company that owes money receives a statutory demand, they have 21 days to either pay the debt or reach an agreement to pay. Failing that, the claimant may apply to bankrupt the individual or wind up the company.

#Credit

Step Change

Charity helping 500,000 people per year to overcome problems with debt, including with hire purchase agreements. See also Business Debtline.
www.stepchange.org

#Credit

Stepped rentals

Where lease payments increase over time, usually on an annual basis. Also referred to as escalating rentals. The technique can help a growing business to afford the lease payments but it comes with the risk that the payments will turn out not to be affordable.

#Contracts

Stipulated loss value

A lease contract may set out how much the lessee must pay to the lessor if the leased equipment is damaged or lost. The contract may stipulate that the loss value will be 'reasonably determined' by the lessor, or it could include a table stipulating absolute values over the course of the contract.

#Contracts

Stocking finance

A revolving loan used to finance stock and secured against it. The borrower retains ownership of the stock unless there is a default.

Some equipment or vehicles dealers who offer leasing options to their customers make use of stocking finance themselves allowing some finance companies to provide both products.

#Alternatives

S

Straight-line depreciation

A pattern of depreciation, where depreciation is calculated based on a constant percentage of the original cost of the asset less the estimated residual value at the start of the lease. The main alternative is reducing balance depreciation.

#Accounting

Strategic alliance

A partnership between a lessor and a manufacturer, for example where the lessor offers 'zero percent' finance deals that are supported by the manufacturer.

#Market

Sub-broking

Where a broker introduces customers to another broker, not to a lessor. Traditionally lessors have not permitted such broker-to-broker business as it is seen as reducing control and therefore causing additional risk. For the FCA regulation of consumer credit, many smaller brokers have now become Appointed Representatives or Agents of larger firms. Most lessors accept these arrangements provided the sub-broker is adequately supervised.

#Intermediaries #Risk

Sub-lease

Where a business leases an asset and then leases it on to another firm. This is usually prohibited by the terms of the original lease as it increases the risk of default, but it is sometimes permitted using an endorsement to the agreement. Assignment or novation techniques may also be used.

#Legal

S

Sub-prime

The least credit-worthy lessees. Tends to refer to consumers or businesses with clear indications of financial difficulties, although precise definitions vary between firms. More commonly used in consumer than business lending. Other customers may be Prime or Near Prime.

#Credit

Subsidy

Where an equipment manufacturer or supplier contributes to the cost of a lease. This may result in a lower interest rate for the lessee or a zero percent finance scheme. It can be achieved through a direct payment to the lessor, or through underwriting part of the lessors' risks.

#Market

Substitutability

Under IFRS 16, if a lease contract allows the lessor to routinely change assets during the agreement, for commercial reasons other than maintenance and repair, this is classified as a service rather than a lease. The relevant rules are complicated and difficult to interpret, but it appears that the IASB's intention was to exclude service-type contracts where the equipment being used is incidental to the value derived by the customer. Whether the Standard achieves that objective remains unclear.

#Accounting

Sum of the digits

An income recognition calculation method used in lessor accounting for finance leases. Also called the 'Rule of 78'. Gross earnings (total rentals receivable less asset cost) are apportioned based on the assumption that the principal is repaid over the term of the lease. On this basis, earnings in each month will be lower than the one before.

The formula used to calculate earnings is based on the number of payments due. Each payment is numbered (1, 2, 3, etc.) and these numbers are summed. For a one-year lease, the sum of the digits is 78, hence the name of the technique. The earnings are then allocated to the periods, with the first being the highest digit (12 for a one-year lease) divided by the sum of the digits multiplied by the earnings. Eleven 78ths is then allocated to the second period, and so on.

The alternative, and more usual, technique is the actuarial method. For operating leases, income is usually recognised on a straight-line basis, i.e. the rentals are spread evenly over the lease term.

#Accounting

Supplier

Any business whose main activity is to sell equipment. Includes resellers and dealers. Suppliers may offer vendor finance to their customers. The finance may be arranged through schemes organised by manufacturers or distributors, or arranged through a broker or direct with a lessor. May also be referred to as a Vendor or Vendor Partner.

#Intermediaries

Supply of goods acts

The Supply of Goods (Implied Terms) Act 1973 and the Supply of Goods and Services Act 1982, together with various other legislation and case law, impose a duty on lessors to ensure that the assets are of satisfactory quality and are reasonably fit for purpose. This tends to be most relevant to consumer finance where the effects of the statutes are clearest.

#Legal

T

Syndicated lease

Large lease made jointly by more than one bank to a borrower. The technique may be used for aircraft, for example.

#Funding

Tax avoidance

Bending the rules of the tax system to gain a tax advantage that was not the intention when the tax law was passed by Parliament, often because the tax advantage had not been foreseen or considered when the legislation was drafted. It is often, but not always, acting against the spirit of the law and can involve contrived, artificial transactions. The popular view of what is tax avoidance has shifted over the years, making some arrangements formerly considered as legitimate appear no longer acceptable.

Unfortunately, many tax avoidance schemes over the years have involved leasing. Most had little to do with genuine leasing activities and have unfairly discredited the industry.

Following successive tightening up loopholes in the leasing tax legislation most tax avoidance schemes involving leasing have disappeared. Furthermore, General Anti-Abuse Rules (GAAR) discourage the development of new schemes and the large advisory firms have now stopped promoting them. As a result, the reputation of the leasing industry in Government has improved, although the leasing tax rules remain long and complicated.

#Tax

Tax-based leasing

Leases where the tax treatment of the agreement is the principal motivation for the choice of financing technique. This implies that the tax treatment is preferential to that of other forms of financing the equipment. In the UK this is now rare as the tax treatment of leases is broadly equivalent to that of other options. In the US, the term tax lease refers to any lease in which the lessor claims the tax allowances.

#Tax

Tax capacity

The taxable profits of a business, against which it can offset capital allowances. If a lessee has no tax capacity, there may be extra benefit in using a lease where the lessor claims the allowances – assuming the lessor has tax capacity itself. The lessor is under no obligation to pass through the tax saving to the lessee, but in the competitive leasing market economic theory would suggest at least part of the benefit will be passed through.

#Tax

Tax point

The date of a transaction for VAT purposes. It is usually the invoice date, unless the invoice is issued 15 days or more after the date the equipment is supplied.

#Tax

Tax variation clause

Where a lease contract stipulates that the rental payments shown are subject to no changes to relevant tax rules. In the event of a change to tax arrangements, the rentals would be varied to, in effect, negate the effect of the change as far as the lessor was concerned.

#Contract #Tax

Technological obsolescence

Where equipment becomes obsolete because technological advances mean that it saves money to replace it with the latest models. Leasing assets provides some protection to the lessee against obsolescence, particularly with shorter leases. Obsolescence reduces residual values for lessors.

#Assets

T

Technology refresh lease

A common selling message for leasing is that it enables the lessee to keep their technology up to date. There is certainly a lot of truth in this, as the fixed minimum-term nature of a lease agreement may encourage lessees to review their equipment every few years and, where relevant, change it. By contrast, for owned equipment inertia or other factors may lead to the equipment being used until it literally dies.

A Technology refresh lease goes a step further than this. It entails a right for the lessee to have their equipment changed, or upgraded, when a new version is released by the manufacturer. Unlike conventional leases where this would incur early cancellation costs, there would be no extra charge. This shifts more of the technology obsolescence risk from the lessee to the lessor. It is quite rare, possibly because most technology updates are software rather than hardware-based, and software updates would already form part of a conventional lease in any case.

#Products

Technology

An evolving term generally used within the leasing sector to describe equipment such as computers, printers and telecommunications. May also be referred to as Information Technology and Communications (ITC). The term tends to be applied to assets for which technological obsolescence is likely. Many lessors will avoid taking residual value risk when leasing technology, offering only full payout leases.

#Assets

Term

The agreed period of the lease. For lease accounting, it is the non-cancellable period adjusted for any option to increase or reduce that period which is very likely to be exercised. IFRS 16 requires the term used for accounting to be adjusted if options are "reasonably certain" to be executed.

#Accounting

T

Term Funding Scheme (TFS)

A new Scheme announced by the Bank of England (BoE) in August 2016. The TFS will allow eligible banks to borrow from the BoE at a low rate in exchange for eligible collateral. The quantity and price of funds available to banks will depend on how much they lend to UK households and businesses. Lending to non-bank credit providers, including specialist leasing companies dealing primarily in finance leases, is eligible. The TFS is replacing the Funding for Lending Scheme.

#Funding

Term loan

Bank loan for a fixed period, with regular interest payments due. It is an alternative to asset finance as a means of financing capital investment.

#Alternatives

Termination fee

The cost to a lessee of terminating the lease before the end of the lease term. The cost of terminating a lease is not usually based on a set fee. The lessee can be liable to pay the full cost of the lease and lessors would face a considerable loss if they waived all of this. Lessors may offer some discount on any interest charges for the remaining period. Specific rules apply if the agreement is consumer credit regulated.

#Contracts

Time order

For regulated agreements, lessees may apply to the courts to be given more time to make their lease payments. Applications for time orders are, however, rare, not least because the FCA Consumer Credit Sourcebook requires firms to treat customers in default or in arrears difficulties with forbearance and due consideration.

#Conduct #Legal

Title

Legal ownership of the asset.

#Legal

Total Cost of Mobility (TCM)

A holistic view of the costs of moving a workforce for the business's activities, whether staff are using company fleet cars, their own cars or public transport. It includes the expense of the owned or leased vehicles alongside other costs including time spent travelling, traffic fines and fleet administration.

#Business

Total Cost of Ownership (TCO)

The sum of the direct and indirect costs of owning an asset over its life. It includes the purchase cost as well as ongoing expenses such as maintenance, support, repairs, training and disposal costs. A robust comparison of ownership versus leasing would consider TCO for each option, particularly for operating leases and contract hire.

#Business

Trade-in

Where a business returns old equipment to the supplier or manufacturer and receives a credit against the cost of replacement of new equipment. If the old equipment has been leased there will be an early settlement of the agreement and a possible rollover to a new contract.

#Business

Treating Customers Fairly (TCF)

All FCA-regulated firms are required to have due regard to the interests of customers and treat them fairly. The FCA provides further guidance on how to treat customers fairly based around six core consumer outcomes. These include, for example, the provision of clear information and keeping customers appropriately informed before, during and after the point of sale.

For regulated business, the FCA's Consumer Credit Rulebook (CONC) contains further detailed rules on conduct of business, hence compliance with CONC must take regulated lessors a long way towards meeting TCF requirements. TCF does not apply directly to unregulated customers, but regulated firms are required to conduct all their business affairs with integrity. It seems difficult to conclude that a firm can therefore treat any customer unfairly, whether regulated or not. Further guidance from the FCA on this point is expected following a consultation held in 2016.

#Conduct

UK Finance

The new trade body for the UK's financial sector. It subsumed the Asset Based Finance Association, the British Bankers' Association, the Council of Mortgage Lenders, Financial Fraud Action UK, Payments UK and the UK Cards Association. It represents nearly 300 of the leading firms providing finance, banking, markets and payments-related services in or from the UK, including most bank-owned lessors. The FLA elected not to join UK Finance when it was established in 2017, maintaining its independence in representing consumer and asset finance lenders.

#Associations

Ultra vires

Latin meaning 'beyond the powers'. In leasing, ultra vires is most commonly used in relation to public sector procurement rules, particularly for schools. In general schools are restricted to using operating rather than finance leases, unless they obtain specific approval to do otherwise (which has proven very difficult to obtain), even though finance leases might be more suitable to a school's needs. Lessors aim to provide agreements that are unequivocally operating leases and obtain written confirmation from the local authority to confirm this to be the case.

#Public sector

U

Underwriting

The process of determining whether or not to offer a lease agreement to a prospective lessee. An underwriter decides whether the lessor should assume the risk of the proposed agreement, in line with the lessor's credit policy and the perceived affordability for the customer.

#Credit

Undisclosed agency

Where the customer enters a lease agreement with a lessor who, in turn, enters a lease agreement with another lessor, the head lessor. The legal owner of the asset is the head-lessor. Many contract hire companies lease cars to their customers which they have themselves leased. The customer is not informed of the existence of the head lessor as their contract is with the contract hire company. The term can also refer to an Agency Purchase arrangement.

#Legal

Unearned finance income

For lease accounting, the difference between the lessor's gross and the net investment in a finance lease. The gross investment is the total of the lease payments to be paid by the lessee plus any expected residual value of the asset. The net investment is the gross investment discounted by the implicit lease rate.

#Accounting

UNIDROIT

The International Institution for the Unification of Private Law, an international organisation based in Rome set up in 1926, which aims to coordinate law between different countries. In 1998 it agreed the Unidroit Convention on International Leasing, intended to promote the legal harmonisation of international leasing.
www.unidroit.org

#Legal

Unincorporated business

A firm that is not a legal entity. Its owners have unlimited personal liability for the activities of the business. Leasing to unincorporated businesses is regulated by the FCA unless the agreement is exempt. All broking to unincorporated businesses is regulated by the FCA.

#Business

Universal document

A lease agreement that does not name a specific lessor until a particular funder has been agreed. It is used by brokers or equipment suppliers to allow them to secure a customer agreement before necessarily having identified the lessor that will fund it. As well as speeding up the process, this avoids brokers having to hold agreements from (potentially) dozens of lessors. However, for funders, using universal documents is sometimes challenging as they will not be able to sign customers up on 'their own' terms and conditions which have been drafted in line with internal policies.

Universal documents are commonly used for small ticket unregulated leases, although for regulated hire purchase agreements FCA rules require the identity of the provider of the credit to be made clear to the customer.

#Contracts

Unregulated agreement

An agreement not regulated under consumer credit law. For the lessor, it will include agreements made with unregulated customers including incorporated businesses and partnerships of 4 or more partners, and agreements that are exempt.

#Conduct

Unsecured loan

A loan provided without the borrower needing to provide any security. It is unusual in the business finance market.

#Alternatives

Upgrade

When a lessee replaces a lease asset with a newer and more useful version. One of the benefits of leasing is that lessees can do this when the lease agreement ends. Upgrading before the end of a lease agreement can, however, result in paying for two assets at the same time, or paying interest on interest, if the settlement figure is rolled into the new lease, even if the effect of extending the term is to make the lease payments similar to those from before the upgrade.

#Contract

Useful life

The expected working life of equipment before it becomes unfit or uneconomical to use, assuming it is maintained in accordance with the manufacturer's guidance. The determinants of useful life vary between types of equipment. They could include intensity of use, pace of technological innovation, and availability of spare parts.

In the early 1990s the UK Office of Fair Trading (OFT) identified problems in the leasing market caused by photocopier leases being written for more than their useful life. The OFT noted this was artificially reducing monthly lease payments and distorting competition. To help address the OFT's concerns members of FLA agreed not to write photocopier leases for more than five years. The FLA Business Finance Code was amended in 2012 to require FLA members to limit leases to expected working life for all types of business equipment, noting this may be shorter than five years.

Also referred to as Economic life.

#Assets

Value Added Tax (VAT)

Value-added tax, a tax on consumption. The tax is charged on a product or service each time it is sold, unless it is exempt or zero-rated.

For leases without a bargain purchase option, VAT is charged on the rental payments. For hire purchase – according to the tax definition being that it is a lease with a bargain purchase option – there are two supplies for VAT purposes. The supply of goods happens when the agreement starts and VAT is chargeable. The supply of credit, being the interest charges, is then exempt from VAT as it is a financial service, hence no further VAT is payable.

As there is no VAT on regular hire purchase payments, this may make the method more attractive for non-VAT registered businesses that cannot offset the VAT they pay against sales. VAT-registered businesses may find it more VAT-efficient to lease assets. VAT recovery on cars leased by businesses is limited to 50% of the lease rentals if there is some private use of the car by employees.

See also Partial exemption.

#Tax

Vanilla lease

Lease with only standard features. Outside of big-ticket leasing, most leases fit this description.

#Contract

Variable rate

An interest rate that may change over time based on an underlying benchmark such as Bank of England official base rate. Although most leases are provided on a fixed rate basis, larger businesses in particular may prefer the lease to be priced on a variable rate especially if the perception is that rates may decrease.

#Finance

V

Variation clause

A clause in a lease agreement allowing the terms of the agreement to change in certain circumstances. The agreement might, for example, allow for a change in the rental payments if there is a change to tax rates.

#Contracts

Vendor

See Supplier.

#Intermediaries

Vendor finance

Financial solutions, most often leasing, offered by vendors to their customers that is not manufacturer (captive) finance. The vendor introduces the customer to either a broker or a funder. Around a quarter of total new asset finance business in the UK market is sold through the vendor channel.

#Market

Warehousing

Where an investor buys the rights to leases in preparation for securitisation of the combined portfolio in the future. The British Business Bank's ENABLE Funding programme is intended to operate as a warehouse facility.

#Funding

Whistleblowers

FCA rules, non-binding for lessors other than those that are part of large banks, that aim to encourage a culture where individuals feel able to raise concerns and challenge poor practice and behaviour. The rules suggest that regulated firms should have procedures in place to allow employees to raise concerns in their firms without fear of being victimised.

#Regulation

W

WRAP

A charity that aims to support more sustainable economies and society. It set up the eQuip Residual Guarantee scheme in 2004 to stimulate investment in the recycling sector. The scheme, which is no longer available for new applications, provided residual value guarantees on plant and machinery to lessors able to provide operating leases to recycling businesses. WRAP determined the eligibility and level of support to be provided to the lessor based on the type of asset and purpose for which the asset will be used. Negotiation and agreement of specific lease terms was left to individual applicants and lessors. WRAP has also funded small-scale farm anaerobic digestion installations, although in 2018 this scheme had closed to new applications pending completion of a review.

#Market

Write-off

Taking an asset, such as the amounts due to be received from a lessee, off the balance sheet, on the basis that the debt will not be paid. The amount written off is charged to the income statement.

#Accounting

Written-down value

The accounting book value of an asset after depreciation and any impairment. Tax written-down value is the original cost of the asset less the capital allowances that have been claimed. The two versions of written-down value should be similar except where the tax system offers enhanced capital allowances. The tax written-down value will then be lower than the accounting book value in the early years of the lease. On disposal of the asset, a balancing charge or allowance is made to reconcile the written-down values. If the tax written-down value is higher than the accounting value, a tax allowance is available. If the tax value is lower than the accounting value, a tax charge is made.

For most business equipment, capital allowances are allowed at 18% per year. For company cars with emissions over 130g/km in 2016, capital allowances are restricted to 8% per year, with no balancing allowance

#Accounting #Tax

Yield

The return earned by the lessor on a lease calculated based on after-tax cashflows. It is stated as a percentage of the original investment in the lease and is calculated over the lease term.

#Operations

Zero percent finance

Particularly during periods of low interest rates, manufacturers may offer subsidised credit, marketed as 'zero percent' finance deals to promote sales. The deals may be provided by captives or by partner finance companies, to whom the manufacturer will pay the subsidy. For consumer credit regulated business it is important to ensure that the Annualised Percentage Rate is actually zero percent.

#Market

Y
Z

Index

All entries are shown with a hashtag (#) label that designates the topic of the item. This is intended to allow the reader to find all items on a topic.

There are 21 topics in total, sorted into six categories as follows:

Business environment

#Alternatives: How businesses can finance assets other than by leasing them.
#Corporate finance: How businesses plan their capital structure.
#Business: All other aspects of the wider business environment pertinent to leasing.

Financial services environment

#Associations: Associations and other groups of firms involved in the leasing market.
#Bodies: Official bodies of particular relevance to the financial services market.
#Funding: How financial services firms raise capital to finance leases.

Leasing market

#Products: Types of leases.
#Public sector: Aspects of leasing specific to public sector customers.
#Market: All other aspects of the leasing market.

Legal

#Contracts: Leasing documentation including lease terms and conditions.
#Legal: All other legal agreements and arrangements pertinent to leasing.

Operations

#Assets: Management of leased equipment and vehicles.
#Risk: Avoiding and managing losses.
#Intermediaries: All aspects of the broker and equipment sales channels.
#Credit: Assessing customers' ability to pay, collecting cash and handling inability to pay
#Operations: All other aspects of lessors' operations.

Regulatory environment

#Accounting: Lease accounting rules and practices.
#Conduct: Financial Conduct Authority regulation of the consumer credit market.
#Prudential: Regulation of the safety and soundness of financial institutions.
#Tax: Tax rules and practices.
#Regulation: All other regulation pertinent to leasing.

Business environment

#Alternatives *(How businesses can finance assets other than by leasing them)*

Advantages of leasing
Alternative finance
Asset based finance
Bill of sale
Chattel mortgage
Credit sale
Crowdfunding
Disadvantages of leasing
Factoring
Instalment credit
Internal finance
Invoice discounting
Mezzanine
Line of credit
Loan
Peer-to-peer finance
Revolving credit
Stocking finance
Term loan
Unsecured loan

#Finance *(How businesses plan their capital structure)*

Basis point
Cashflow
Cost of capital
Discount rate
Discounted cashflow
Flat rate
Hurdle rate
Interest
Lease vs. buy
Net present value
Nominal rate

Present value
Rate
Real interest rate
Spread
Variable rate

#Business *(All other aspects of the wider business environment pertinent to leasing)*

Ethics
Fintech
Internet of Things
Limited company
Limited Liability Partnership
Listed company
Open banking
Partnership
Professionalism
Project finance
Public Limited Company
Recession
Sharing economy
Small and Medium-sized Enterprises
Social responsibility
Special Purpose Vehicle
Start-up
Total Cost of Mobility
Total Cost of Ownership
Trade-in
Unincorporated business

Financial services environment

#Associations *(Associations and other groups of firms involved in the leasing market)*

Asset Based Finance Association
Asset Finance Professionals Association
British Banking Association
British Vehicle Rental and Leasing Association
Captives Forum
Consumer Credit Trade Association
Equipment Leasing and Finance Association
Equipment Leasing Association
Equipment Leasing and Finance Foundation
Finance and Leasing Association
Finance Houses Association
Financial Intermediaries and Brokers Association
International Finance and Leasing Association
Leaseurope
Leasing Broker Federation
Leasing Foundation
National Association of Commercial Finance Brokers
UK Finance

#Bodies *(Official bodies of particular relevance to the financial services market)*

Bank of England
Bank of International Settlements
Basel Committee
British Business Bank
Chartered Institute of Credit Management
Department for Business, Energy and Industrial Strategy
Educational Funding Agency
European Central Bank
European Data Warehouse
European Investment Bank
European Investment Fund
Financial Conduct Authority

Financial Ombudsman Service
HM Treasury
Joint Money Laundering Steering Group

#Funding *(How financial services firms raise capital to finance leases)*

Asset-Backed Commercial Paper
Asset-Backed Securities
Block discounting
Bond
Capital market
Club loan
Collateral risk
Collaterised Lease Equipment Obligations
European Data Warehouse
Funding
Funding for Lending Scheme
Institutional investors
Interest
Interest rate risk
Money market
Over-collateralisation
Private equity
Secondary market
Securitisation
Special Purpose Vehicle
Syndicated lease
Term Funding Scheme
Warehousing

Leasing market

#Products *(Types of leases)*

Back to back lease
Conditional sale
Contract hire
Finance lease
Fixed term rental
Full payout lease
Full service lease
Hire Purchase
Lease purchase
Lease with sales agency
Lease with secondary rental
Minimum period lease
Open-ended lease
Operating lease
Sale and leaseback
Technology refresh lease

#Public sector *(Aspects of leasing specific to public sector customers)*

Capital charges
Crown Commercial Services
Educational and Skills Funding Agency
Financial Reporting Advisory Board
Healthcare Financial Management Association
Managed Equipment Service
NHS Supply Chain
Ultra Vires

#Market *(All other aspects of the leasing market)*

Advantages of leasing
Aircraft leasing
Asset finance
Asset Finance 50
Asset Finance 500

Asset Finance International
BEN
Big-ticket
Blind discount
Blockchain
Captive lessor
Circular economy
Container leasing
Cross-border leasing
Export leasing
Finance House
Finance House Base Rate
Fleet
Funder
Head lessor
High value leasing
Independent lessor
Interest free
International leasing
Lease
Leasing
Leasing Life
Leasing World
Middle ticket lease
Non-recourse funding
Penetration rate
Portfolio
Prime lenders
Recourse
Regional Growth Fund
Relationship lending
Renewables
Retail bank
Rolling Stock Operating Company
Sales-aid
Shariah leasing
Small ticket lease
Soft loan
Software

Strategic alliance
Subsidy
Vendor finance
WRAP
Zero percent finance

Legal

#Contracts *(leasing documentation including lease terms and conditions)*

Additions
Advance lease payments
Annual service fee
Balloon payment
Bargain purchase option
Bargain renewal option
Break option
Commitment letter
Consumables
Contingent rentals
Continuation
Co-terminous agreement
Covenants
Default interest
Deposit
Drawdown
e-signature
Early settlement
Endorsement
Equipment schedule
Evergreen lease
Extension rental
Fair value
Fees
Fixed rate
Floating charge
Holdback
Holiday
Insurance
Lease payments
Lease rate factor
Lease term
Lessee
Lessor

Leveraged lease
Liability
Maintenance
Minimum term
Options
Option to purchase
Payment frequency
Peppercorn rents/rentals
Personal guarantee
Primary lease period
Principal
Profile
Purchase option
Rear-end loading
Refinancing
Renewal option
Rentals
Restrictive covenant
Return conditions
Roll-over
Schedule
Secondary period
Security
Security deposit
Settlement
Soft costs
Stage payment
Stepped rentals
Stipulated loss value
Tax variation clause
Termination fee
Upgrade
Universal document
Vanilla lease
Variation clause

#Legal *(all other legal agreements and arrangements pertinent to leasing)*

Acceptance certificate
Agency agreement
Agency purchase
Assignment
Bailment
Common law
Credit
Disclosed agency
Facility letter
Fixed charge
Head lessor
Hell or high water
Hire
Indemnity
Landlord's waiver
Liability
Master lease
Novation
Pre-lease agreement
Promissory note
Repudiation
Retention
Sub-lease
Supply of Goods acts
Time order
Title
Undisclosed agency
Unidroit

Operations

#Assets *(Management of leased equipment and vehicles)*

Appraisal
Asset
Asset disposal
Asset register
Buy-back
Call option
DIMS
Economic life
Fixtures
Hard asset
HPI
Inspection
Intangible asset
Maintenance
Manufacturer buy-back
Multi-financing
Off-lease equipment
Purchase price
Put option
Repossession
Repossession
Residual value
Residual value guarantee
Residual value insurance
Return conditions
Salvage value
Soft asset
Technological obsolescence
Technology
Useful life

#Risk *(Avoiding and managing losses)*

Acceptance certificate
Administration

Asset register
Audit
Bad debt
Bankruptcy
Business risk
CIFAS
Claims Management Company
Collateral risk
Construction & Agricultural Equipment Security and
Registration Scheme
Consumables
Cost of risk
County Court Judgement
Credit risk
Dual financing
Dun & Bradstreet Critical Intelligence System
Embezzlement
Floating charge
Fraud
Holdback
Insolvency
Insolvency Practitioner
Inspection
Interest rate risk
Invoice fraud
Kickback
Lien
Liquidation
Multi-financing
National Crime Agency
National Fraud Intelligence Bureau
Operational risk
Payout
Repossession
Residual risk
Residual value guarantee
Residual value insurance
Section 75 claim
Security

Security deposit
Side-letter
Sub-broking

#Intermediaries *(All aspects of the broker and equipment sales channels)*

Broker
Clawbacks
Commissions
Dealers
Difference in Charges commission
Distributors
Introducer Appointed Representative
Own-book
Remarketing agreement
Repurchase agreement
Reseller
Sub-broking
Supplier
Vendor

#Credit *(Assessing customers' ability to pay, collecting cash and handling inability to pay)*

Acceptance ratio
Administration order
Arrears
Bad debt
Cashflow
Business Debtline
Collections
Commercial CAIS
Credit rating
Credit risk
Default
Default interest
Delinquent receivable
Direct debit

Guarantee
Near-prime
Non-performing loan
Open banking
Personal guarantee
Prime
Receivables
Rejection
Standing order
Statutory Demand
Step Change
Sub-prime
Underwriting

#**Operations** *(All other aspects of lessors' operations)*

Artificial Intelligence
Big data analytics
Conversion rate
Cost of risk
Cost/income
End-of-life functions
Finance Houses Diploma
In-life functions
Loan to value ratio
Leaseurope Index
Margin
Payment Card Industry Data Security Standard
Payout
Origination
Outsourcing
Ratio analysis
Return on assets
Return on equity
Run-off
Yield

Regulatory environment

#Accounting *(Lease accounting rules and practices)*

Accelerated depreciation
Accounting standards
Accounting Standards Board
Actuarial method
Amortisation
Audit
Balance sheet
Bargain renewal option
Capital employed
Capital expenditure
Capitalised value
Contingent rentals
Continuation
Credit loss
Deferred taxation
Depreciation
Earnings before Interest and Tax
Economic owner
Equity in a lease
European Financial Reporting Advisory Group
Fair value
Finance lease
Financial Accounting Standards Board
Financial Reporting Advisory Board
Financial Reporting Council
Financial Reporting Standards
Fixed assets
Fixtures
Gross investment in the lease
IAS 17
IFRS 9
IFRS 15
IFRS 16
Implicit lease rate
Initial direct costs

Lease term
Margin
Market rental
Minimum lease payments
Net book value
Net investment in the lease
Ninety percent test
Off-balance sheet
Operating lease
Operating profit/loss
Profitability
Provisions
Reducing balance depreciation
Return on capital employed
Revenue
Right-of-Use Asset
Rule of 78
Service
Short-term lease
SSAP 21
Straight-line depreciation
Substitutability
Sum of the digits
Term
Unearned finance income
Write-off
Written-down value

#Conduct *(Financial Conduct Authority regulation of the consumer credit market)*

Affordability
Agent
Annualised Percentage Rate
Appointed Representative
Conduct of business
Consumer credit
Consumer Credit Act
Consumer Credit Sourcebook

Credit
Debt adjusting
Debt counselling
Fees
Financial Conduct Authority
Financial Ombudsman Service
High net worth
Hire
Introducer Appointed Representative
Regulated agreement
SECCI
Time order
Treating Customers Fairly
Unregulated agreement

#**Prudential** *(Regulation of the safety and soundness of financial institutions)*

Advanced Internal Ratings Based Approach
Bank of International Settlements
Basel Committee
Capital adequacy
Credit institution
European Central Bank
Loss Given Default
Operational risk
Probability of Default
Prudential regulation
Regulatory capital
Risk weighted assets
Standardised approach

#**Tax** *(Tax rules and practices)*

Annual Investment Allowance
Capital allowances
Carry forward
Corporate interest restriction rules
Corporation tax

Deferred taxation
Direct tax
Double-dip lease
Economic owner
Enhanced capital allowances
Fittings
Fixtures
Foreign Exchange Tax Compliance Act
Hire Purchase
HM Revenue & Customs
Long funding lease
Operating lease
Partial exemption
Place of supply
Plant and machinery
Salary sacrifice
Self-billing
Short lease
Tax avoidance
Tax capacity
Tax point
Tax-based leasing
Tax variation clause
Value Added Tax
Written-down value

#Regulation *(All other regulation pertinent to leasing.)*

Anti-Money Laundering
Bank Referral Scheme
Data protection
General Data Protection Regulation
Information Commissioner's Office
Joint Money Laundering Steering Group
Know Your Customer
Money laundering
Politically Exposed Persons checks
Sanctions checks
Section 75 claim

Self-regulation
Shadow banking
Whistleblowers

Abbreviations

AIRB	Advanced Internal Ratings Based approach
AML	Anti-Money Laundering
ICO	Information Commissioner's Office
JMLSG	Joint Money Laundering Steering Group
KYC	Know Your Customer
FRS	Financial Reporting Standard
AIA	Annual Investment Allowance
AML	Anti-Money Laundering
AR	Appointed Representative
ABCP	Asset-Backed Commercial Paper
ABS	Asset-Backed Securities
ABFA	Asset Based Finance Association
AF-PA	Asset Finance Professionals Association
BIS	Bank of International Settlements
BBA	British Bankers' Association
BBB	British Business Bank
BVRLA	British Vehicle Rental and Leasing Association
CCJ	County Court Judgement
CICM	Chartered Institute of Credit Management
CESAR	Construction & Agricultural Equipment Security and Registration Scheme
CCTA	Consumer Credit Trade Association
CCS	Crown Commercial Service
BEIS	Department for Business, Energy and Industrial Strategy
EBIT	Earnings before Interest and Tax
ESFA	Education and Skills Funding Agency
ELFA	Equipment Leasing and Finance Association
ECB	European Central Bank
EDW	European Data Warehouse
EFRAG	European Financial Reporting Advisory Group
EIB	European Investment Bank
EIF	European Investment Fund
FLA	Finance and Leasing Association
FASB	Financial Accounting Standards Board
FATCA	Foreign Account Tax Compliance Act
FCA	Financial Conduct Authority

FOS	Financial Ombudsman Service
FRAB	Financial Reporting Advisory Board
FRC	Financial Reporting Council
FLS	Funding for Lending Scheme
GDPR	General Data Protection Regulation
HMRC	HM Revenue and Customs
HMT	HM Treasury
ICO	Information Commissioner's Office
IFLA	International Finance and Leasing Association
IoT	Internet of Things
IAR	Introducer Appointed Representative
JMLSG	Joint Money Laundering Steering Group
KYC	Know Your Customer
LLP	Limited Liability Partnership
LGD	Loss Given Default
MES	Managed Equipment Service
NACFB	National Association of Commercial Finance Brokers
NPV	Net Present Value
PCI DSS	Payment Card Industry Data Security Standard
PD	Probability of Default
PLC	Public Limited Company
ROU	Right-of-Use
ROSCO	Rolling Stock Operating Company
SMEs	Small and Medium-sized Enterprises
TCM	Total Cost of Mobility
TCO	Total Cost of Ownership
TCF	Treating Customers Fairly
VAT	Value Added Tax

Short quiz

1) **What is a Secondary lease period?**
   a) The period of use of the leased asset covered by the second lease payment
   b) The period of use of the leased asset after the agreed primary lease period (minimum term)
   c) The period of use of an asset by a second lessee, after the asset's return from the first lessee
   d) The remaining length of a lease that has been sold to a second lessor

2) **Which of these types of leases should result in a Profile of constant Lease payments?**
   a) Fixed rate lease
   b) Lease with a balloon payment
   c) Lease based on a variable rate
   d) Lease with stepped rentals

3) **Which of the following is <u>not</u> a typical Advantage of leasing?**
   a) Additional source of finance for a business
   b) Lower cost of equipment
   c) Facility cannot be withdrawn during the term
   d) Avoid residual value risk

4) **When might a lease be Ultra vires?**
   a) When the party signing the lease does not have the legal power or authority to do so
   b) A lease that does not meet the Financial Conduct Authority's handbook requirements
   c) Any contract that is outside of the definition of a lease for IFRS 16
   d) A lease that has continued beyond the agreed primary lease period (minimum term)

5) **Which of the following is <u>not</u> a trade publication?**
   a) Asset Finance International
   b) Leasing World

   c)   Leasing Life

   d)   Leaseurope

6) Which of the following is a tax, not an accounting term?

   a)   Right-of-Use Asset

   b)   Short-term lease

   c)   Long funding lease

   d)   Finance lease

7) Which of the following is not a Financial Conduct Authority regulated activity?

   a)   Credit broking

   b)   Debt adjusting

   c)   Capital adequacy

   d)   Debt counselling

8) Which accounting standard introduced the term 'Right-of-use' Assets?

   a)   IFRS 16

   b)   IFRS 15

   c)   IAS 17

   d)   FRS 102

9) Which does a lessor report as its Revenue from finance leases?

   a)   Finance income

   b)   Gross cash receipts

   c)   Net investment in the lease

   d)   Depreciation

10) Which of the following is the name of a common term in a Lease agreement?

   a)   Undisclosed agency

   b)   Landlord's waiver

   c)   Early settlement

   d)   Agency agreement

11) What is a Deposit?

   a)   The first regular rental payment

b) Payment towards the cost of the equipment
c) An amount held by the lessor to cover any damages
d) A rental payment paid before the start of the agreed primary lease period (minimum term)

12) **What is a typical cost of risk (loan loss provisions as a percentage of average portfolio) for European lessors?**
   a) 0.05%
   b) 5%
   c) 15%
   d) 0.5%

13) **What is a typical cost/income ratio (operating expenses excluding interest as a percentage of operating income including net interest) for European lessors?**
   a) 25%
   b) 45%
   c) 65%
   d) 85%

14) **What is a typical Return on assets (net profit before tax as a percentage of average portfolio size over a period) for European lessors?**
   a) 2%
   b) 0.2%
   c) 20%
   d) 40%

15) **The top ten UK leasing firms have what approximate market share according to the Asset Finance 50?**
   a) 88%
   b) 18%
   c) 38%
   d) 58%

16) **Which of the following is <u>not</u> treated as a lease cost in the accounts of a Contract hire user?**
   a) Lease rental payments
   b) Depreciation

c) Maintenance
d) Insurance

17) **According to the DIMS test, which of the following most suggests an asset is suitable for leasing?**
    a) It cannot be moved
    b) It is a soft asset
    c) It has a short life_
    d) It is identifiable

18) **Which of these is not usually a lease for accounting purposes?**
    a) Hire purchase
    b) Conditional sale
    c) Contract hire
    d) Asset based finance

19) **If a lessor uses a third party to manage its portfolio of leases, this is called:**
    a) Novation
    b) Outsourcing
    c) Assignment
    d) Refinancing

20) **Which of the following is a type of option for a lessor?**
    a) Break
    b) Purchase
    c) Renewal_
    d) Put

21) **Where is the term 'leasing' defined in UK law?**
    a) Consumer Credit Act
    b) Financial Services Act
    c) Nowhere
    d) Finance Bill 2017

22) **From a tax perspective, how might a lessee without taxable profits benefit from leasing?**
    a) Enhanced Capital allowances

b) First year Capital allowances
c) Operating lease
d) Finance lease

23) What types of firms must use IFRS 16?
a) All companies
b) Listed companies
c) Firms with international subsidiaries
d) Firms with off-balance sheet operating leases

24) What type of fraud prevention information is shared using CIFAS?
a) Suspected financial crime
b) Confirmed corporate fraud
c) Confirmed financial crime
d) Suspected money laundering

25) If a broker funds a deal itself rather than introduce it to a lender, what is this called?
a) Own book
b) Origination
c) Refinancing
d) Retention

26) Which is the better indicator of an Operating lease, rather than a Finance lease?
a) No option to purchase
b) Lease period covers most of the economic life of the asset
c) Value of lease payments is close to the cost of the asset
d) Option to extend the lease at a low rate

27) In general, leasing is seen as an activity unlikely to be used for money laundering, but which of these factors might indicate a higher than normal risk?
a) Rental payments being collected by direct debit from a UK business account
b) Leasing of assets that are difficult to resell at a high value

   c)   A request to reimburse overpayments to a third party

   d)   Leasing by an established business

28) What is the name of a leasing contract that does not initially name a specific lessor?

   a)   Schedule

   b)   Agency agreement

   c)   Vanilla lease_

   d)   Universal document

29) Which of the following is <u>not</u> an example of Operational risk?

   a)   Fire at the lessors' offices

   b)   Increase in defaults

   c)   Software faults in the lessor's systems

   d)   A data breach

30) Which of the following is a type of Fraud?

   a)   Clawback

   b)   Double-dip lease

   c)   Multi-financing

   d)   Soft asset

Quiz answers are on page 204

Select Bibliography

An Economic Analysis of the Financial Leasing Industry, Cyril Tomkins, Julian Lowe & Eleanor Morgan, Saxon House, 1979

Asset Finance Leasing Handbook, Richard Grant & David Gent, Woodhead-Faulkner, 1992

Elements of Finance and Leasing, Alastair Day, Financial World Publishing, 2000

Commercial Hiring and Leasing, John Adams, Butterworths, 1989

Equipment Leasing, Peter K. Nevitt & Frank J. Fabozzi, Dow-Jones Irwin, 1988

Equipment Leasing in the UK, HMSO, 1995

European Leasing Handbook, Marijan Nemet, NWB Verlag GmbH & Co Kg, 2011

Finance leasing: a guide for lessees in the UK, Graham Hubbard. Institute of Cost and Management Accountants, 1980

Handbook of Equipment Leasing, Richard M. Contino, American Management Association, 1996

HP and Leasing Finance, D. C. Gardner, FT Pitman, 1996

Leasing, David Wainman, Sweet & Maxwell, 1991

Leasing and Asset Finance, Chris Boobyer (Editor), Euromoney, 2003

Leasing, Tom M. Clark, McGraw Hill, 1978

Leasing Finance, Tom Clark (Ed), Euromoney Books, 1990

The Leasing Handbook, Derek R. Soper & Ewen Cameron, McGraw-Hill, 1999

Asset Finance 50

The following data is taken from the first edition of the Asset Finance 50 (AF50) rankings survey published by Asset Finance Policy and Asset Finance International (AFI).

The survey is based on audited and publicly available accounts or other published information to ensure it is compliant with competition law and regulations. It aims to include the top 50 UK business equipment and fleet lessors based on their accounts that are filed at Companies House.

The data shown below is from the 2018 edition that was based on the latest information filed online at Companies House at February 2018. It is estimated the Asset Finance 50 includes between 90% and 95% of the total market.

The rankings are based on the lessor's net investment in business equipment leasing. It includes all asset finance agreements where the asset is owned by the lessor during the life of the agreement.

For finance leases and hire purchase, the results show the present value of total receivables less unearned (deferred) income and impairments.

For operating leases, the tables show the undiscounted minimum contracted future lease payments. Where there is no operating lease disclosure, the table shows 50% of the balance sheet carrying amount of assets used for operating leases as a proxy for the minimum contracted future lease payments.

Several banks have leasing business in multiple parts of their groups, including wholly or part-owned specialist leasing subsidiaries or divisions. The Banking subsidiaries version table shows only the banking groups' leasing-specific subsidiaries. The Banking groups version table show the groups' total leasing activities.

The total net investment in leasing for the top 50 firms reported in the 2018 edition was £37.1 billion.

Asset Finance 50
Banking subsidiaries version

Rank	Name	£m
1	Lombard	4,664
2	HSBC	2,464
3	Lex	2,446
4	LeasePlan	2,364
5	Close Brothers	2,017
6	BNP Paribas	1,876
7	DLL	1,532
8	Barclays	1,428
9	Aldermore	1,340
10	Hitachi Capital	1,309
11	European Rail Finance	1,279
12	Angel Trains	1,132
13	Porterbrook	1,038
14	Siemens	948
15	Alphabet	941
16	Santander	858
17	Investec	785
18	Arval UK	784
19	ALD	731
20	Societe Generale	725
21	JCB	690
23	Clydesdale	565
22	PACCAR	533
24	VFS	509
25	Scania	402
26	NIIB	339
27	GE Capital	303

Rank	Name	£m
28	Caterpillar	258
29	Paragon Bank	250
30	PEAC	250
31	BLME	244
32	Xerox Finance	198
33	Allied Irish Banks	182
34	Grenke	160
35	Ricoh Capital	141
36	IBM	136
37	Shawbrook	121
38	Secure Trust	117
39	Metro Bank	115
40	Hampshire Trust	112
41	SQN	104
42	Haydock	94
43	United Trust	85
44	Liberty Leasing	80
45	Shire Leasing	77
46	Maxxia	76
47	Asset Advantage	71
48	Arkle Finance	70
49	PCF Bank	70
50	Bibby Leasing	68

Fuller details of the methodology used, and important limitations of the survey are shown in the report available from the AFI website (*www.assetfinanceinternational.com*).

Asset Finance 50
Banking groups version

This table includes all reported leasing receivables of the groups

Rank	Name	£ m
1	RBS	9,364
2	HSBC	5,922
3	Lloyds	5,468
4	LeasePlan	2,364
5	Close Brothers	2,017
6	BNP Paribas	1,876
7	DLL	1,532
8	Barclays	1,607
9	Aldermore	1,340
10	Hitachi Capital	1,309

Fuller details of the methodology used, and important limitations of the survey are shown in the report available from the AFI website (*www.assetfinanceinternational.com*).

Request for Input

Any suggestions for improvements to the terms covered and additional terms that could be included in future editions would be welcome.

Please contact Julian Rose at *Julian@assetfinancepolicy.co.uk*.

About the Authors

Julian Rose is the founder and director of Asset Finance Policy Limited, an independent regulatory affairs consultancy uniquely dedicated to serving the UK asset finance industry.

From 2008 to 2014 he was Head of Asset Finance at the Finance & Leasing Association. His previous experience spans regulation (Financial Reporting Council, Competition Commission), management consulting (PwC, KPMG) and industry (NCR, United Parcel Service). He is a Chartered Management Accountant and has Masters Degrees in management (Boston University) and competition and regulation (University of East Anglia).

Established in March 2014, Asset Finance Policy has supported more than 100 clients ranging from sole trader asset finance brokers to European banks.

Asset Finance International commented in 2014:

Rose has, for the last six years, been a staunch supporter of asset lending and has played his part in lobbying long and hard for asset lenders to receive a higher profile and relevance amongst government decision makers... Rose's preferred approach has always been to adopt a firm, but courteous and logical, approach towards persuading those with an uncertain appreciation of the asset lending to see the error of their ways... Rose's single-minded yet gentlemanly approach to the future welfare of the asset finance sector coupled with his compendious knowledge of the industry will be a sore miss to the FLA. It should, however, ensure his sound onward-going career as an industry consultant.

"I have known and worked with Julian for many years. Over that period Julian has always demonstrated excellent attention to detail combined with an ability to try and see the issues and the challenges that the industry faces from all perspectives. As such, Julian's work outputs are always well thought through, relevant and strategically meaningful. This work is no exception." George Ashworth, Managing Director Asset Finance, Santander UK plc

www.assetfinancepolicy.co.uk

Stephen Bassett is currently Chairman of AF-PA Trust, a charity which raises funds in the UK asset finance and leasing sector; he also holds various non-executive positions in the industry.

Mr Bassett is a Master of Business Administration (MBA) and also holds a Finance House Diploma; he has had some 45 years of experience in many and varied aspects of this market, particularly in equipment leasing.

Latterly (2009-2017) Mr Bassett was Managing Director of Arkle Finance Limited, the leasing subsidiary of Weatherbys, a private bank with roots stretching back to 1770, and he oversaw a substantial growth in the portfolio during this period.

Prior to that Mr Bassett was Managing Director of Wyse Leasing Plc, a long established and well known finance broker, until its sale to a larger international specialist in finance and technology.

From 2001 until its sale to Siemens Financial Services Mr Bassett served as Chief Operations Officer with Broadcastle Plc, a Licensed Banking Institution quoted on the London Stock Exchange.

Previous employments have included Lloyds & Scottish Finance; Schroder Leasing and Lombard North Central.

Mr Bassett was a member of the Royal Naval Reserve for some fifteen years, obtaining a Queen's Commission and achieving the rank of Lieutenant Commander. He received his education at Harrow County School for Boys.

Reviews of the first edition

Julian Rose's A to Z of Leasing and Asset Finance is likely to prove a revelation for the industry. Produced in association with Arkle Finance, it contains a comprehensive list of industry terms and definitions together with a description of the range of agreement types which exist, as well as the general legal and regulatory frameworks surrounding such agreements.

As such it is a must for new entrants into the industry as well as a valuable aide memoire for current practitioners. Rose's wide experience of the industry ensures that the explanations offered in the book describe the various ways in which some terms are used for different purposes, including for accounting (covering the new IFRS 16), taxation, and in law and regulation.

The A to Z of Leasing and Asset Finance fills a gap in the asset finance industry's reservoir of knowledge that has grown significantly since the great recession.

As Carl D'Ammassa, group managing director – business finance, Aldermore Bank, explains in the Foreword: "Where has all the training gone? That valuable insight from experts that passes on their knowledge and experience; that action of teaching that transfers skills and enables the student to competently execute their duties or tasks.

"It's fair to say that little has been done in our industry throughout the financial crisis to ensure the diligent transfer of knowledge and expertise."

He adds: "Competency and skill in how we transact is a pre-requisite in this growing market and changing regulatory environment. Borrowers expect us to support them with precision and expertise. That's why the reinvigoration, perhaps better described as restoration, of critical knowledge transfer and training from industry experts is vital."

Thus Rose's book, which comes with 165 pages packed with definitions and explanatory detail. This writer was especially impressed with a most valuable cross-referencing index which serves to allow readers to find all items on a particular topic – a most helpful tool for those seeking to broaden their knowledge of a topic. Indeed he was delighted to discover clarifying explanations of little understood terms such as Partial Exemption – and the often forgotten but valuable Sum of the Digits.

Brian Rogerson, Asset Finance International

Hot off the press, "A-Z of Leasing and Asset Finance" by Julian Rose, is a neat handy-sized volume of some 150 pages. The book was produced in association with Arkle Finance Limited, with Stephen Basset, Arkle's MD, noted as Principal Contributor. It has a Foreword penned by Carl D'Ammassa, Group MD of Business Finance at Aldermore Bank PLC, and an endorsement from George Ashworth, Santander UK plc, who calls it, "The what's what of asset finance".

The bulk of the book is like a dictionary, devoted to definitions of leasing, asset finance and associated financial terms, listed in alphabetical order. There are also useful short sections giving a brief history of leasing, decade by decade, since the 1960s, and an explanation of common abbreviations. The Index, always a sign of a professional publishing effort, is excellent and comprehensive, and has an additional alternative index that references all the definitions by six categories (e.g. Business Environment, Legal, Operations, etc), further subdivided into 21 Topic areas (e.g. Funding, Public Sector, Assets, Risk, etc). The Bibliography shows impressive diligence on the part of the author, listing books on leasing going back to the 1970s. To gauge the appetite for such a book we took the liberty of showing it to MDs and CEOs we met during the month, not exactly scientific market research, but enough to persuade us that there is a market for this book with lessors and brokers, as a training resource and reference guide for their new starters and junior people. On several occasions PR and Communications people attending those meetings also examined the book and said that it would be useful to them as they were not asset finance experts but regularly had to deal with leasing "jargon". The definitions are very reader-friendly, for example, "Bad Debt" is explained as "Amounts owed to a lessor no longer expected to be paid. They are written-off as losses for accounting purposes. A more common term used in the industry is default". Another good example is "Loss Given Default (LGD)" explained as "Ratio of the loss due to the default of a borrower to the amount outstanding at default. The LGD for leasing is measured after any benefit obtained from selling the asset is realised".

But being reader-friendly doesn't mean it's dumbed down by any means, and weightier expressions like "Capital Adequacy" and "Partial Exemption" get a full page to themselves. Julian concludes his book with a "Request for Input" saying that any suggestions for improvements, or additional terms that could be included in future editions would be welcome. So here's a few suggestions from the editor. During the course of reviewing the book, a couple of words came to mind, expressions frequently used in our trade with a good few years of usage behind them, such as "Run-off", "Money-over-money" or "Sale and HP-back" though other expressions like "Hybrid funder" or "Super-broker" may be too new and possibly transient to feature just yet.

Jan Szmigin, Leasing World

Julian Rose's book plugs a notable gap in the educational market for concise and to the point definitions of the key aspects of leasing and asset finance. Highly recommend for anyone trying to get their heads around the terminology and nuances of the market.

Managing Director, international investment management firm (via Amazon)

Quiz Answers

1	B	16	B
2	A	17	D
3	B	18	D
4	A	19	B
5	D	20	D
6	C	21	C
7	C	22	C
8	A	23	B
9	A	24	C
10	C	25	A
11	B	26	A
12	D	27	C
13	B	28	D
14	A	29	B
15	D	30	C